"After utilizing toolkits from Tl
threats within my organization to which I was completely unaware. Using my team's knowledge as a competitive advantage, we now have superior systems that save time and energy."

"As a new Chief Technology Officer, I was feeling unprepared and inadequate to be successful in my role. I ordered an IT toolkit Sunday night and was prepared Monday morning to shed light on areas of improvement within my organization. I no longer felt overwhelmed and intimidated, I was excited to share what I had learned."

"I used the questionnaires to interview members of my team. I never knew how many insights we could produce collectively with our internal knowledge."

"I usually work until at least 8pm on weeknights. The Art of Service questionnaire saved me so much time and worry that Thursday night I attended my son's soccer game without sacrificing my professional obligations."

"After purchasing The Art of Service toolkit, I was able to identify areas where my company was not in compliance that could have put my job at risk. I looked like a hero when I proactively educated my team on the risks and presented a solid solution."

"I spent months shopping for an external consultant before realizing that The Art of Service would allow my team to consult themselves! Not only did we save time not catching a consultant up to speed, we were able to keep our company information and industry secrets confidential."

"Everyday there are new regulations and processes in my industry. The Art of Service toolkit has kept me ahead by using AI technology to constantly update the toolkits and address emerging needs."

"I customized The Art of Service toolkit to focus specifically on the concerns of my role and industry. I didn't have to waste time with a generic self-help book that wasn't tailored to my exact situation."

"Many of our competitors have asked us about our secret sauce. When I tell them it's the knowledge we have in-house, they never believe me. Little do they know The Art of Service toolkits are working behind the scenes."

"One of my friends hired a consultant who used the knowledge gained working with his company to advise their competitor. Talk about a competitive disadvantage! The Art of Service allowed us to keep our knowledge from walking out the door along with a huge portion of our budget in consulting fees."

"Honestly, I didn't know what I didn't know. Before purchasing The Art of Service, I didn't realize how many areas of my business needed to be refreshed and improved. I am so relieved The Art of Service was there to highlight our blind spots."

"Before The Art of Service, I waited eagerly for consulting company reports to come out each month. These reports kept us up to speed but provided little value because they put our competitors on the same playing field. With The Art of Service, we have uncovered unique insights to drive our business forward."

"Instead of investing extensive resources into an external consultant, we can spend more of our budget towards pursuing our company goals and objectives...while also spending a little more on corporate holiday parties."

"The risk of our competitors getting ahead has been mitigated because The Art of Service has provided us with a 360-degree view of threats within our organization before they even arise."

Work Planning And Estimation
Complete Self-Assessment Guide

Table of Contents

About The Art of Service

The Art of Service, Business Process Architects since 2000, is dedicated to helping stakeholders achieve excellence.

Defining, designing, creating, and implementing a process to solve a stakeholders challenge or meet an objective is the most valuable role… In EVERY group, company, organization and department.

Unless you're talking a one-time, single-use project, there should be a process. Whether that process is managed and implemented by humans, AI, or a combination of the two, it needs to be designed by someone with a complex enough perspective to ask the right questions.

Someone capable of asking the right questions and step back and say, 'What are we really trying to accomplish here? And is there a different way to look at it?'

With The Art of Service's Self-Assessments, we empower people who can do just that — whether their title is marketer, entrepreneur, manager, salesperson, consultant, Business Process Manager, executive assistant, IT Manager, CIO etc... —they are the people who rule the future. They are people who watch the process as it happens, and ask the right questions to make the process work better.

Contact us when you need any support with this Self-Assessment and any help with templates, blue-prints and examples of standard documents you might need:

https://theartofservice.com
support@theartofservice.com

Included Resources - how to access

Included with your purchase of the book is the Work Planning

And Estimation Self-Assessment Spreadsheet Dashboard which contains all questions and Self-Assessment areas and auto-generates insights, graphs, and project RACI planning - all with examples to get you started right away.

How? Simply send an email to
access@theartofservice.com
with this books' title in the subject to get the Work Planning And Estimation Self Assessment Tool right away.

The auto reply will guide you further, you will then receive the following contents with New and Updated specific criteria:

- The latest quick edition of the book in PDF

- The latest complete edition of the book in PDF, which criteria correspond to the criteria in...

- The Self-Assessment Excel Dashboard, and...

- Example pre-filled Self-Assessment Excel Dashboard to get familiar with results generation

- In-depth specific Checklists covering the topic

- Project management checklists and templates to assist with implementation

INCLUDES LIFETIME SELF ASSESSMENT UPDATES

Every self assessment comes with Lifetime Updates and Lifetime Free Updated Books. Lifetime Updates is an industry-first feature which allows you to receive verified self assessment updates, ensuring you always have the most accurate information at your fingertips.

Get it now- you will be glad you did - do it now, before you forget.

Send an email to **access@theartofservice.com** with this books' title in the subject to get the Work Planning And Estimation Self Assessment Tool right away.

Purpose of this Self-Assessment

This Self-Assessment has been developed to improve understanding of the requirements and elements of Work Planning And Estimation, based on best practices and standards in business process architecture, design and quality management.

It is designed to allow for a rapid Self-Assessment to determine how closely existing management practices and procedures correspond to the elements of the Self-Assessment.

The criteria of requirements and elements of Work Planning And Estimation have been rephrased in the format of a Self-Assessment questionnaire, with a seven-criterion scoring system, as explained in this document.

In this format, even with limited background knowledge of Work Planning And Estimation, a manager can quickly review existing operations to determine how they measure up to the standards. This in turn can serve as the starting point of a 'gap analysis' to identify management tools or system elements that might usefully be implemented in the organization to help improve overall performance.

How to use the Self-Assessment

On the following pages are a series of questions to identify to what extent your Work Planning And Estimation initiative is complete in comparison to the requirements set in standards.

To facilitate answering the questions, there is a space in front of each question to enter a score on a scale of '1' to '5'.

1 Strongly Disagree

2 Disagree

3 Neutral

4 Agree

5 Strongly Agree

Read the question and rate it with the following in front of mind:

**'In my belief,
the answer to this question is clearly defined'.**

There are two ways in which you can choose to interpret this statement;

1. how aware are you that the answer to the question is clearly defined
2. for more in-depth analysis you can choose to gather evidence and confirm the answer to the question. This obviously will take more time, most Self-Assessment users opt for the first way to interpret the question and dig deeper later on based on the outcome of the overall Self-Assessment.

A score of '1' would mean that the answer is not clear at all, where a '5' would mean the answer is crystal clear and defined. Leave emtpy when the question is not applicable or you don't want to answer it, you can skip it without affecting your score. Write your score in the space provided.

After you have responded to all the appropriate statements in each section, compute your average score for that section, using the formula provided, and round to the nearest tenth. Then transfer to the corresponding spoke in the Work Planning And Estimation Scorecard on the second next page of the Self-Assessment.

Your completed Work Planning And Estimation Scorecard will give you a clear presentation of which Work Planning And Estimation areas need attention.

Work Planning And Estimation Scorecard Example

Example of how the finalized Scorecard can look like:

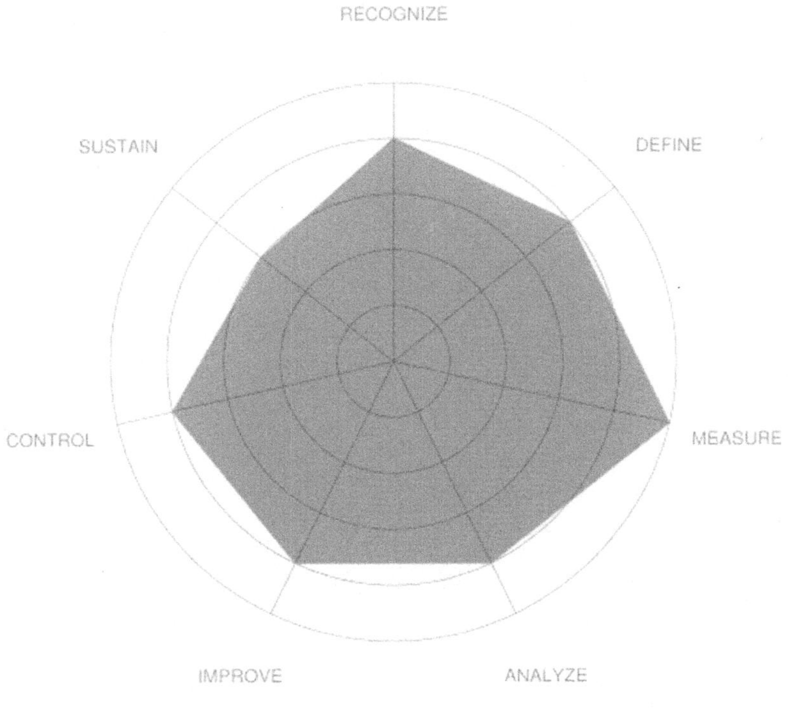

Work Planning And Estimation Scorecard

Your Scores:

BEGINNING OF THE SELF-ASSESSMENT:

CRITERION #1: RECOGNIZE

INTENT: Be aware of the need for change. Recognize that there is an unfavorable variation, problem or symptom.

In my belief, the answer to this question is clearly defined:

5 Strongly Agree

4 Agree

3 Neutral

2 Disagree

1 Strongly Disagree

1. What are your needs in relation to Work Planning and Estimation skills, labor, equipment, and markets?
<--- Score

2. How do you take a forward-looking perspective in identifying Work Planning and Estimation research related to market response and models?
<--- Score

3. What creative shifts do you need to take?
<--- Score

4. Who needs what information?
<--- Score

5. What needs to be done?
<--- Score

6. When a Work Planning and Estimation manager recognizes a problem, what options are available?
<--- Score

7. What are the clients issues and concerns?
<--- Score

8. For your Work Planning and Estimation project, identify and describe the business environment, is there more than one layer to the business environment?
<--- Score

9. Are there any revenue recognition issues?
<--- Score

10. Which needs are not included or involved?
<--- Score

11. What information do users need?
<--- Score

12. Are there regulatory / compliance issues?
<--- Score

13. What else needs to be measured?
<--- Score

14. Have you identified your Work Planning and Estimation key performance indicators?
<--- Score

15. Consider your own Work Planning and Estimation project, what types of organizational problems do you think might be causing or affecting your problem, based on the work done so far?
<--- Score

16. What are the expected benefits of Work Planning and Estimation to the stakeholder?
<--- Score

17. Who defines the rules in relation to any given issue?
<--- Score

18. What is the recognized need?
<--- Score

19. Does Work Planning and Estimation create potential expectations in other areas that need to be recognized and considered?
<--- Score

20. Whom do you really need or want to serve?
<--- Score

21. What Work Planning and Estimation coordination do you need?
<--- Score

22. What training and capacity building actions are needed to implement proposed reforms?

<--- Score

23. How do you identify the kinds of information that you will need?
<--- Score

24. Where is training needed?
<--- Score

25. Have you identified key milestones?
<--- Score

26. What Work Planning and Estimation events should you attend?
<--- Score

27. What is the problem or issue?
<--- Score

28. Are losses recognized in a timely manner?
<--- Score

29. How many trainings, in total, are needed?
<--- Score

30. What is the extent or complexity of the Work Planning and Estimation problem?
<--- Score

31. Do you recognize Work Planning and Estimation achievements?
<--- Score

32. How do you identify subcontractor relationships?
<--- Score

33. Why is this needed?
<--- Score

34. Are problem definition and motivation clearly presented?
<--- Score

35. Who needs to know about Work Planning and Estimation?
<--- Score

36. What would happen if Work Planning and Estimation weren't done?
<--- Score

37. Who needs budgets?
<--- Score

38. What tools and technologies are needed for a custom Work Planning and Estimation project?
<--- Score

39. What vendors make products that address the Work Planning and Estimation needs?
<--- Score

40. Would you recognize a threat from the inside?
<--- Score

41. What situation(s) led to this Work Planning and Estimation Self Assessment?
<--- Score

42. Who needs to know?
<--- Score

43. What should be considered when identifying available resources, constraints, and deadlines?
<--- Score

44. Are your goals realistic? Do you need to redefine your problem? Perhaps the problem has changed or maybe you have reached your goal and need to set a new one?
<--- Score

45. What extra resources will you need?
<--- Score

46. Does your organization need more Work Planning and Estimation education?
<--- Score

47. What is the smallest subset of the problem you can usefully solve?
<--- Score

48. Are employees recognized or rewarded for performance that demonstrates the highest levels of integrity?
<--- Score

49. Do you need different information or graphics?
<--- Score

50. Who else hopes to benefit from it?
<--- Score

51. Which issues are too important to ignore?
<--- Score

52. Who should resolve the Work Planning and

Estimation issues?
<--- Score

53. How are the Work Planning and Estimation's objectives aligned to the group's overall stakeholder strategy?
<--- Score

54. Is the need for organizational change recognized?
<--- Score

55. How do you recognize an Work Planning and Estimation objection?
<--- Score

56. Where do you need to exercise leadership?
<--- Score

57. Are there Work Planning and Estimation problems defined?
<--- Score

58. Is the quality assurance team identified?
<--- Score

59. Think about the people you identified for your Work Planning and Estimation project and the project responsibilities you would assign to them, what kind of training do you think they would need to perform these responsibilities effectively?
<--- Score

60. Which information does the Work Planning and Estimation business case need to include?
<--- Score

61. Will a response program recognize when a crisis occurs and provide some level of response?
<--- Score

62. To what extent would your organization benefit from being recognized as a award recipient?
<--- Score

63. Are there recognized Work Planning and Estimation problems?
<--- Score

64. What are the timeframes required to resolve each of the issues/problems?
<--- Score

65. What does Work Planning and Estimation success mean to the stakeholders?
<--- Score

66. What do employees need in the short term?
<--- Score

67. How much are sponsors, customers, partners, stakeholders involved in Work Planning and Estimation? In other words, what are the risks, if Work Planning and Estimation does not deliver successfully?
<--- Score

68. Will new equipment/products be required to facilitate Work Planning and Estimation delivery, for example is new software needed?
<--- Score

69. How are you going to measure success?

<--- Score

70. What are the stakeholder objectives to be achieved with Work Planning and Estimation?
<--- Score

71. How does it fit into your organizational needs and tasks?
<--- Score

72. As a sponsor, customer or management, how important is it to meet goals, objectives?
<--- Score

73. What is the problem and/or vulnerability?
<--- Score

74. What needs to stay?
<--- Score

75. Do you need to avoid or amend any Work Planning and Estimation activities?
<--- Score

76. Does the problem have ethical dimensions?
<--- Score

77. When do certain tasks need to occur?
<--- Score

78. Are employees recognized for desired behaviors?
<--- Score

79. Are there any specific expectations or concerns about the Work Planning and Estimation team, Work Planning and Estimation itself?

<--- Score

80. What Work Planning and Estimation capabilities do you need?
<--- Score

81. Are controls defined to recognize and contain problems?
<--- Score

82. What problems are you facing and how do you consider Work Planning and Estimation will circumvent those obstacles?
<--- Score

Add up total points for this section:
_____ = Total points for this section

Divided by: ______ (number of statements answered) = ______
Average score for this section

Transfer your score to the Work Planning and Estimation Index at the beginning of the Self-Assessment.

CRITERION #2: DEFINE:

INTENT: Formulate the stakeholder problem. Define the problem, needs and objectives.

In my belief, the answer to this question is clearly defined:

5 Strongly Agree

4 Agree

3 Neutral

2 Disagree

1 Strongly Disagree

1. Are required metrics defined, what are they?
<--- Score

2. Is the team sponsored by a champion or stakeholder leader?
<--- Score

3. Have the customer needs been translated into specific, measurable requirements? How?

<--- Score

4. Is special Work Planning and Estimation user knowledge required?
<--- Score

5. Has everyone on the team, including the team leaders, been properly trained?
<--- Score

6. Is the team equipped with available and reliable resources?
<--- Score

7. Are project objectives and performance criteria defined?
<--- Score

8. How do you manage scope?
<--- Score

9. Is Work Planning and Estimation linked to key stakeholder goals and objectives?
<--- Score

10. How would you define Work Planning and Estimation leadership?
<--- Score

11. Are project scope assumptions and exclusions defined?
<--- Score

12. What are the Work Planning and Estimation use cases?
<--- Score

13. Are roles and responsibilities formally defined?
<--- Score

14. Is there a clear Work Planning and Estimation case definition?
<--- Score

15. Is the work to date meeting requirements?
<--- Score

16. Have all basic functions of Work Planning and Estimation been defined?
<--- Score

17. How can the value of Work Planning and Estimation be defined?
<--- Score

18. How do you manage unclear Work Planning and Estimation requirements?
<--- Score

19. What are the rough order estimates on cost savings/opportunities that Work Planning and Estimation brings?
<--- Score

20. Is data collected and displayed to better understand customer(s) critical needs and requirements.
<--- Score

21. How does the Work Planning and Estimation manager ensure against scope creep?
<--- Score

22. Is Work Planning and Estimation required?
<--- Score

23. How are consistent Work Planning and Estimation definitions important?
<--- Score

24. Is scope creep really all bad news?
<--- Score

25. Is the team adequately staffed with the desired cross-functionality? If not, what additional resources are available to the team?
<--- Score

26. Are there different segments of customers?
<--- Score

27. Will a Work Planning and Estimation production readiness review be required?
<--- Score

28. Are audit criteria, scope, frequency and methods defined?
<--- Score

29. Is a fully trained team formed, supported, and committed to work on the Work Planning and Estimation improvements?
<--- Score

30. Do you have organizational privacy requirements?
<--- Score

31. How was the 'as is' process map developed,

reviewed, verified and validated?
<--- Score

32. What are the record-keeping requirements of Work Planning and Estimation activities?
<--- Score

33. What is a worst-case scenario for losses?
<--- Score

34. What are the requirements for audit information?
<--- Score

35. Are improvement team members fully trained on Work Planning and Estimation?
<--- Score

36. What scope to assess?
<--- Score

37. How would you define the culture at your organization, how susceptible is it to Work Planning and Estimation changes?
<--- Score

38. Has anyone else (internal or external to the group) attempted to solve this problem or a similar one before? If so, what knowledge can be leveraged from these previous efforts?
<--- Score

39. Are customer(s) identified and segmented according to their different needs and requirements?
<--- Score

40. What baselines are required to be defined and

managed?
<--- Score

41. Has a team charter been developed and communicated?
<--- Score

42. Is there any additional Work Planning and Estimation definition of success?
<--- Score

43. Will team members perform Work Planning and Estimation work when assigned and in a timely fashion?
<--- Score

44. Is the team formed and are team leaders (Coaches and Management Leads) assigned?
<--- Score

45. Is it clearly defined in and to your organization what you do?
<--- Score

46. Will team members regularly document their Work Planning and Estimation work?
<--- Score

47. Who is gathering Work Planning and Estimation information?
<--- Score

48. What was the context?
<--- Score

49. What are the tasks and definitions?

<--- Score

50. Scope of sensitive information?
<--- Score

51. Has/have the customer(s) been identified?
<--- Score

52. How and when will the baselines be defined?
<--- Score

53. Is there a completed SIPOC representation, describing the Suppliers, Inputs, Process, Outputs, and Customers?
<--- Score

54. What is in scope?
<--- Score

55. Who is gathering information?
<--- Score

56. What critical content must be communicated – who, what, when, where, and how?
<--- Score

57. Are the Work Planning and Estimation requirements complete?
<--- Score

58. What is the definition of Work Planning and Estimation excellence?
<--- Score

59. What is the scope of Work Planning and Estimation?

<--- Score

60. Has the improvement team collected the 'voice of the customer' (obtained feedback – qualitative and quantitative)?
<--- Score

61. What is out of scope?
<--- Score

62. When are meeting minutes sent out? Who is on the distribution list?
<--- Score

63. Is there a critical path to deliver Work Planning and Estimation results?
<--- Score

64. Is full participation by members in regularly held team meetings guaranteed?
<--- Score

65. How do you build the right business case?
<--- Score

66. What Work Planning and Estimation services do you require?
<--- Score

67. Are stakeholder processes mapped?
<--- Score

68. Are project objectives and performance criteria well defined?
<--- Score

69. Are different versions of process maps needed to account for the different types of inputs?
<--- Score

70. Which is the least desirable practice in the case of a distributed team?
<--- Score

71. If substitutes have been appointed, have they been briefed on the Work Planning and Estimation goals and received regular communications as to the progress to date?
<--- Score

72. What would be the goal or target for a Work Planning and Estimation's improvement team?
<--- Score

73. What gets examined?
<--- Score

74. Does the team have regular meetings?
<--- Score

75. Is the current 'as is' process being followed? If not, what are the discrepancies?
<--- Score

76. What scope do you want your strategy to cover?
<--- Score

77. Is the scope of Work Planning and Estimation defined?
<--- Score

78. Is the Work Planning and Estimation scope

complete and appropriately sized?
<--- Score

79. What sort of initial information to gather?
<--- Score

80. How did the Work Planning and Estimation manager receive input to the development of a Work Planning and Estimation improvement plan and the estimated completion dates/times of each activity?
<--- Score

81. Who defines (or who defined) the rules and roles?
<--- Score

82. How do you gather requirements?
<--- Score

83. What are the dynamics of the communication plan?
<--- Score

84. What intelligence can you gather?
<--- Score

85. What are the Roles and Responsibilities for each team member and its leadership? Where is this documented?
<--- Score

86. What is the scope of the Work Planning and Estimation effort?
<--- Score

87. In what way can you redefine the criteria of choice clients have in your category in your favor?

<--- Score

88. Is the improvement team aware of the different versions of a process: what they think it is vs. what it actually is vs. what it should be vs. what it could be?
<--- Score

89. What is out-of-scope initially?
<--- Score

90. How do you gather the stories?
<--- Score

91. When is the estimated completion date?
<--- Score

92. Are customers identified and high impact areas defined?
<--- Score

93. Do the problem and goal statements meet the SMART criteria (specific, measurable, attainable, relevant, and time-bound)?
<--- Score

94. How do you keep key subject matter experts in the loop?
<--- Score

95. What are the compelling stakeholder reasons for embarking on Work Planning and Estimation?
<--- Score

96. Are resources adequate for the scope?
<--- Score

97. Has a high-level 'as is' process map been completed, verified and validated?
<--- Score

98. Do you all define Work Planning and Estimation in the same way?
<--- Score

99. Who approved the Work Planning and Estimation scope?
<--- Score

100. What are the Work Planning and Estimation tasks and definitions?
<--- Score

101. What happens if Work Planning and Estimation's scope changes?
<--- Score

102. The political context: who holds power?
<--- Score

103. Are all requirements met?
<--- Score

104. What system do you use for gathering Work Planning and Estimation information?
<--- Score

105. How to estimate the required team size of agile teams?
<--- Score

106. How will the Work Planning and Estimation team and the group measure complete success of Work

Planning and Estimation?
<--- Score

107. How are the project requirements collected?
<--- Score

108. How often are the team meetings?
<--- Score

109. When is/was the Work Planning and Estimation start date?
<--- Score

110. Have all of the relationships been defined properly?
<--- Score

111. Has the Work Planning and Estimation work been fairly and/or equitably divided and delegated among team members who are qualified and capable to perform the work? Has everyone contributed?
<--- Score

112. Does the scope remain the same?
<--- Score

113. Are there any constraints known that bear on the ability to perform Work Planning and Estimation work? How is the team addressing them?
<--- Score

114. What customer feedback methods were used to solicit their input?
<--- Score

115. What is the scope of the Work Planning and

Estimation work?
<--- Score

116. Are approval levels defined for contracts and supplements to contracts?
<--- Score

117. What is the scope?
<--- Score

118. Is Work Planning and Estimation currently on schedule according to the plan?
<--- Score

119. Is the Work Planning and Estimation scope manageable?
<--- Score

120. Is there a completed, verified, and validated high-level 'as is' (not 'should be' or 'could be') stakeholder process map?
<--- Score

121. Who are the Work Planning and Estimation improvement team members, including Management Leads and Coaches?
<--- Score

122. What information should you gather?
<--- Score

123. How have you defined all Work Planning and Estimation requirements first?
<--- Score

124. What Work Planning and Estimation

requirements should be gathered?
<--- Score

125. What specifically is the problem? Where does it occur? When does it occur? What is its extent?
<--- Score

126. What knowledge or experience is required?
<--- Score

127. Are accountability and ownership for Work Planning and Estimation clearly defined?
<--- Score

128. How is the team tracking and documenting its work?
<--- Score

129. Is there regularly 100% attendance at the team meetings? If not, have appointed substitutes attended to preserve cross-functionality and full representation?
<--- Score

130. Are team charters developed?
<--- Score

131. Has a project plan, Gantt chart, or similar been developed/completed?
<--- Score

132. Is there a Work Planning and Estimation management charter, including stakeholder case, problem and goal statements, scope, milestones, roles and responsibilities, communication plan?
<--- Score

133. What are the boundaries of the scope? What is in bounds and what is not? What is the start point? What is the stop point?
<--- Score

134. How do you catch Work Planning and Estimation definition inconsistencies?
<--- Score

135. Has the direction changed at all during the course of Work Planning and Estimation? If so, when did it change and why?
<--- Score

136. Do you have a Work Planning and Estimation success story or case study ready to tell and share?
<--- Score

137. What is in the scope and what is not in scope?
<--- Score

138. What constraints exist that might impact the team?
<--- Score

139. What key stakeholder process output measure(s) does Work Planning and Estimation leverage and how?
<--- Score

140. How will variation in the actual durations of each activity be dealt with to ensure that the expected Work Planning and Estimation results are met?
<--- Score

Add up total points for this section:
_____ = Total points for this section

Divided by: ______ (number of statements answered) = ______ Average score for this section

Transfer your score to the Work Planning and Estimation Index at the beginning of the Self-Assessment.

CRITERION #3: MEASURE:

INTENT: Gather the correct data.
Measure the current performance and
evolution of the situation.

In my belief, the answer to this
question is clearly defined:

5 Strongly Agree

4 Agree

3 Neutral

2 Disagree

1 Strongly Disagree

1. What are allowable costs?
<--- Score

2. How are costs allocated?
<--- Score

3. Have impacts to commercial and/or recreational usage been adequately assessed/allowed for?
<--- Score

4. What are hidden Work Planning and Estimation quality costs?
<--- Score

5. Are you aware of what could cause a problem?
<--- Score

6. What is the Work Planning and Estimation business impact?
<--- Score

7. Do interdependencies exist between tasks and/or other projects that may impact estimates?
<--- Score

8. What disadvantage does this cause for the user?
<--- Score

9. Are the Work Planning and Estimation benefits worth its costs?
<--- Score

10. What does losing customers cost your organization?
<--- Score

11. Should a project team start by focusing on high risk features that could derail the entire project?
<--- Score

12. Was a business case (cost/benefit) developed?
<--- Score

13. Is there an opportunity to verify requirements?

<--- Score

14. Have you made assumptions about the shape of the future, particularly its impact on your customers and competitors?
<--- Score

15. What are predictive Work Planning and Estimation analytics?
<--- Score

16. What relevant entities could be measured?
<--- Score

17. Are there measurements based on task performance?
<--- Score

18. Which Work Planning and Estimation impacts are significant?
<--- Score

19. When a disaster occurs, who gets priority?
<--- Score

20. What causes innovation to fail or succeed in your organization?
<--- Score

21. What happens if cost savings do not materialize?
<--- Score

22. How can you reduce the costs of obtaining inputs?
<--- Score

23. Who is involved in verifying compliance?

<--- Score

24. Are appropriate historical cost data used in the estimate?
<--- Score

25. What are the costs of reform?
<--- Score

26. What can be used to verify compliance?
<--- Score

27. How will success or failure be measured?
<--- Score

28. The approach of traditional Work Planning and Estimation works for detail complexity but is focused on a systematic approach rather than an understanding of the nature of systems themselves, what approach will permit your organization to deal with the kind of unpredictable emergent behaviors that dynamic complexity can introduce?
<--- Score

29. How does cost-to-serve analysis help?
<--- Score

30. Do the benefits outweigh the costs?
<--- Score

31. How do you measure efficient delivery of Work Planning and Estimation services?
<--- Score

32. How will you measure success?
<--- Score

33. What is an unallowable cost?
<--- Score

34. How will the Work Planning and Estimation data be analyzed?
<--- Score

35. Is the solution cost-effective?
<--- Score

36. Are there any easy-to-implement alternatives to Work Planning and Estimation? Sometimes other solutions are available that do not require the cost implications of a full-blown project?
<--- Score

37. What does your operating model cost?
<--- Score

38. Does management have the right priorities among projects?
<--- Score

39. How do your measurements capture actionable Work Planning and Estimation information for use in exceeding your customers expectations and securing your customers engagement?
<--- Score

40. What is measured? Why?
<--- Score

41. What is the total fixed cost?
<--- Score

42. What is your Work Planning and Estimation quality cost segregation study?
<--- Score

43. What is the total cost related to deploying Work Planning and Estimation, including any consulting or professional services?
<--- Score

44. What causes mismanagement?
<--- Score

45. Have you included everything in your Work Planning and Estimation cost models?
<--- Score

46. What are your primary costs, revenues, assets?
<--- Score

47. What are your customers expectations and measures?
<--- Score

48. How can you reduce costs?
<--- Score

49. Are supply costs steady or fluctuating?
<--- Score

50. Do the costs and benefits justify continuing?
<--- Score

51. How do you aggregate measures across priorities?
<--- Score

52. What would be the total cost of the project

until completion?
<--- Score

53. How do you stay flexible and focused to recognize larger Work Planning and Estimation results?
<--- Score

54. Why a Work Planning and Estimation focus?
<--- Score

55. Why do the measurements/indicators matter?
<--- Score

56. Do you effectively measure and reward individual and team performance?
<--- Score

57. How do you quantify and qualify impacts?
<--- Score

58. What are the current costs of the Work Planning and Estimation process?
<--- Score

59. How can you measure Work Planning and Estimation in a systematic way?
<--- Score

60. How is the value delivered by Work Planning and Estimation being measured?
<--- Score

61. What is the root cause(s) of the problem?
<--- Score

62. How is performance measured?

<--- Score

63. What do you measure and why?
<--- Score

64. How do you control the overall costs of your work processes?
<--- Score

65. Do you have any cost Work Planning and Estimation limitation requirements?
<--- Score

66. Was a life-cycle cost analysis performed?
<--- Score

67. What is the cause of any Work Planning and Estimation gaps?
<--- Score

68. What methods are feasible and acceptable to estimate the impact of reforms?
<--- Score

69. How do you measure success?
<--- Score

70. How do you measure lifecycle phases?
<--- Score

71. Where is it measured?
<--- Score

72. Are there competing Work Planning and Estimation priorities?
<--- Score

73. What are the estimated costs of proposed changes?
<--- Score

74. How do you verify the authenticity of the data and information used?
<--- Score

75. What does a Test Case verify?
<--- Score

76. What is the cost of rework?
<--- Score

77. How frequently do you verify your Work Planning and Estimation strategy?
<--- Score

78. What measurements are possible, practicable and meaningful?
<--- Score

79. Which prioritization technique did the team follow?
<--- Score

80. What do people want to verify?
<--- Score

81. What does verifying compliance entail?
<--- Score

82. What are the success criteria for a methodology while performing process analysis?
<--- Score

83. What kind of analytics data will be gathered?
<--- Score

84. How can you measure the performance?
<--- Score

85. Are actual costs in line with budgeted costs?
<--- Score

86. What are the uncertainties surrounding estimates of impact?
<--- Score

87. Do you verify that corrective actions were taken?
<--- Score

88. Is it possible to estimate the impact of unanticipated complexity such as wrong or failed assumptions, feedback, etcetera on proposed reforms?
<--- Score

89. Among the Work Planning and Estimation product and service cost to be estimated, which is considered hardest to estimate?
<--- Score

90. How do you measure variability?
<--- Score

91. How do you prevent mis-estimating cost?
<--- Score

92. How do you verify and develop ideas and innovations?

<--- Score

93. Who pays the cost?
<--- Score

94. How is progress measured?
<--- Score

95. Will Work Planning and Estimation have an impact on current business continuity, disaster recovery processes and/or infrastructure?
<--- Score

96. Which costs should be taken into account?
<--- Score

97. Is a follow-up focused external Work Planning and Estimation review required?
<--- Score

98. How will effects be measured?
<--- Score

99. What are the types and number of measures to use?
<--- Score

100. Have external interfaces been defined and adequate costs allowed for within the estimate?
<--- Score

101. Are you taking your company in the direction of better and revenue or cheaper and cost?
<--- Score

102. How do you verify if Work Planning and

Estimation is built right?
<--- Score

103. How do you verify the Work Planning and Estimation requirements quality?
<--- Score

104. What prioritization methods have you used on different projects?
<--- Score

105. How will you measure your Work Planning and Estimation effectiveness?
<--- Score

106. How will measures be used to manage and adapt?
<--- Score

107. What are your key Work Planning and Estimation organizational performance measures, including key short and longer-term financial measures?
<--- Score

108. Are missed Work Planning and Estimation opportunities costing your organization money?
<--- Score

109. What are the costs and benefits?
<--- Score

110. How do you focus on what is right -not who is right?
<--- Score

111. What are the costs of delaying Work Planning and

Estimation action?
<--- Score

112. Are the activity durations in the schedule consistent with the estimated cost?
<--- Score

113. What evidence is there and what is measured?
<--- Score

114. What causes extra work or rework?
<--- Score

115. Are Work Planning and Estimation vulnerabilities categorized and prioritized?
<--- Score

116. What details are required of the Work Planning and Estimation cost structure?
<--- Score

117. What causes investor action?
<--- Score

118. Are the units of measure consistent?
<--- Score

119. What are the Work Planning and Estimation key cost drivers?
<--- Score

120. How long to keep data and how to manage retention costs?
<--- Score

121. What harm might be caused?

<--- Score

122. How will costs be allocated?
<--- Score

123. Have design-to-cost goals been established?
<--- Score

124. What are the strategic priorities for this year?
<--- Score

125. What potential environmental factors impact the Work Planning and Estimation effort?
<--- Score

126. At what cost?
<--- Score

127. Do you aggressively reward and promote the people who have the biggest impact on creating excellent Work Planning and Estimation services/ products?
<--- Score

128. How are you verifying it?
<--- Score

129. What users will be impacted?
<--- Score

130. What would it cost to replace your technology?
<--- Score

131. What are the Work Planning and Estimation investment costs?
<--- Score

132. How do you know what a project will cost?
<--- Score

133. What could cause delays in the schedule?
<--- Score

134. What would be a real cause for concern?
<--- Score

135. How to cause the change?
<--- Score

136. Does the Work Planning and Estimation task fit the client's priorities?
<--- Score

137. How can a Work Planning and Estimation test verify your ideas or assumptions?
<--- Score

Add up total points for this section:
_____ = Total points for this section

Divided by: ______ (number of statements answered) = ______
Average score for this section

Transfer your score to the Work Planning and Estimation Index at the beginning of the Self-Assessment.

CRITERION #4: ANALYZE:

INTENT: Analyze causes, assumptions and hypotheses.

In my belief, the answer to this question is clearly defined:

5 Strongly Agree

4 Agree

3 Neutral

2 Disagree

1 Strongly Disagree

1. What did the team gain from developing a sub-process map?
<--- Score

2. What is the complexity of the output produced?
<--- Score

3. Have the problem and goal statements been updated to reflect the additional knowledge gained from the analyze phase?

<--- Score

4. Are Work Planning and Estimation changes recognized early enough to be approved through the regular process?
<--- Score

5. What is the output?
<--- Score

6. What qualifications are necessary?
<--- Score

7. What were the crucial 'moments of truth' on the process map?
<--- Score

8. Can you add value to the current Work Planning and Estimation decision-making process (largely qualitative) by incorporating uncertainty modeling (more quantitative)?
<--- Score

9. How do you measure the operational performance of your key work systems and processes, including productivity, cycle time, and other appropriate measures of process effectiveness, efficiency, and innovation?
<--- Score

10. Is the Work Planning and Estimation process severely broken such that a re-design is necessary?
<--- Score

11. Was a cause-and-effect diagram used to explore the different types of causes (or sources of variation)?

<--- Score

12. How do your work systems and key work processes relate to and capitalize on your core competencies?
<--- Score

13. What Work Planning and Estimation data should be managed?
<--- Score

14. Is data and process analysis, root cause analysis and quantifying the gap/opportunity in place?
<--- Score

15. Is the suppliers process defined and controlled?
<--- Score

16. Were there any improvement opportunities identified from the process analysis?
<--- Score

17. What tools were used to narrow the list of possible causes?
<--- Score

18. What were the financial benefits resulting from any 'ground fruit or low-hanging fruit' (quick fixes)?
<--- Score

19. Who will gather what data?
<--- Score

20. How do you implement and manage your work processes to ensure that they meet design requirements?

<--- Score

21. Is the final output clearly identified?
<--- Score

22. What is the Work Planning and Estimation Driver?
<--- Score

23. Is the gap/opportunity displayed and communicated in financial terms?
<--- Score

24. What process should you select for improvement?
<--- Score

25. What is the cost of poor quality as supported by the team's analysis?
<--- Score

26. What is the Value Stream Mapping?
<--- Score

27. Who gets your output?
<--- Score

28. Did any additional data need to be collected?
<--- Score

29. An organizationally feasible system request is one that considers the mission, goals and objectives of the organization, key questions are: is the Work Planning and Estimation solution request practical and will it solve a problem or take advantage of an opportunity to achieve company goals?
<--- Score

30. How has the Work Planning and Estimation data been gathered?
<--- Score

31. How do mission and objectives affect the Work Planning and Estimation processes of your organization?
<--- Score

32. What conclusions were drawn from the team's data collection and analysis? How did the team reach these conclusions?
<--- Score

33. Have any additional benefits been identified that will result from closing all or most of the gaps?
<--- Score

34. Do you have the authority to produce the output?
<--- Score

35. Were Pareto charts (or similar) used to portray the 'heavy hitters' (or key sources of variation)?
<--- Score

36. What internal processes need improvement?
<--- Score

37. Was a detailed process map created to amplify critical steps of the 'as is' stakeholder process?
<--- Score

38. Where is Work Planning and Estimation data gathered?
<--- Score

39. How will the data be checked for quality?
<--- Score

40. Do your contracts/agreements contain data security obligations?
<--- Score

41. What Work Planning and Estimation data should be collected?
<--- Score

42. How is the way you as the leader think and process information affecting your organizational culture?
<--- Score

43. How do you ensure that the Work Planning and Estimation opportunity is realistic?
<--- Score

44. When should a process be art not science?
<--- Score

45. What information qualified as important?
<--- Score

46. Has data output been validated?
<--- Score

47. Record-keeping requirements flow from the records needed as inputs, outputs, controls and for transformation of a Work Planning and Estimation process, are the records needed as inputs to the Work Planning and Estimation process available?
<--- Score

48. Is the performance gap determined?

<--- Score

49. How many input/output points does it require?
<--- Score

50. Is your current project date driven or feature driven?
<--- Score

51. How is the data gathered?
<--- Score

52. What kind of crime could a potential new hire have committed that would not only not disqualify him/her from being hired by your organization, but would actually indicate that he/she might be a particularly good fit?
<--- Score

53. What are the disruptive Work Planning and Estimation technologies that enable your organization to radically change your business processes?
<--- Score

54. What are your Work Planning and Estimation processes?
<--- Score

55. Is pre-qualification of suppliers carried out?
<--- Score

56. What controls do you have in place to protect data?
<--- Score

57. What process improvements will be needed?
<--- Score

58. Who will facilitate the team and process?
<--- Score

59. How often will data be collected for measures?
<--- Score

60. Do quality systems drive continuous improvement?
<--- Score

61. What output to create?
<--- Score

62. Where is the data coming from to measure compliance?
<--- Score

63. What qualifications are needed?
<--- Score

64. What types of data do your Work Planning and Estimation indicators require?
<--- Score

65. What other jobs or tasks affect the performance of the steps in the Work Planning and Estimation process?
<--- Score

66. Are all staff in core Work Planning and Estimation subjects Highly Qualified?
<--- Score

67. Identify an operational issue in your organization, for example, could a particular task be done more quickly or more efficiently by Work Planning and Estimation?
<--- Score

68. What are your key performance measures or indicators and in-process measures for the control and improvement of your Work Planning and Estimation processes?
<--- Score

69. Are all team members qualified for all tasks?
<--- Score

70. What is your organizations system for selecting qualified vendors?
<--- Score

71. How can risk management be tied procedurally to process elements?
<--- Score

72. Do staff qualifications match your project?
<--- Score

73. What are the best opportunities for value improvement?
<--- Score

74. What data is gathered?
<--- Score

75. What are the processes for audit reporting and management?
<--- Score

76. Is there any way to speed up the process?
<--- Score

77. Were any designed experiments used to generate additional insight into the data analysis?
<--- Score

78. Do your employees have the opportunity to do what they do best everyday?
<--- Score

79. Are all activities with negative total float drive the project completion date?
<--- Score

80. How will the Work Planning and Estimation data be captured?
<--- Score

81. Who qualifies to gain access to data?
<--- Score

82. Where can you get qualified talent today?
<--- Score

83. What are the personnel training and qualifications required?
<--- Score

84. What are your best practices for minimizing Work Planning and Estimation project risk, while demonstrating incremental value and quick wins throughout the Work Planning and Estimation project lifecycle?
<--- Score

85. A compounding model resolution with available relevant data can often provide insight towards a solution methodology; which Work Planning and Estimation models, tools and techniques are necessary?
<--- Score

86. Is there a strict change management process?
<--- Score

87. Do you understand your management processes today?
<--- Score

88. How do you identify specific Work Planning and Estimation investment opportunities and emerging trends?
<--- Score

89. What are the Work Planning and Estimation design outputs?
<--- Score

90. Do several people in different organizational units assist with the Work Planning and Estimation process?
<--- Score

91. What are your outputs?
<--- Score

92. How does the organization define, manage, and improve its Work Planning and Estimation processes?
<--- Score

93. How difficult is it to qualify what Work Planning

and Estimation ROI is?
<--- Score

94. What are your current levels and trends in key Work Planning and Estimation measures or indicators of product and process performance that are important to and directly serve your customers?
<--- Score

95. What are the Work Planning and Estimation business drivers?
<--- Score

96. Is the required Work Planning and Estimation data gathered?
<--- Score

97. What will drive Work Planning and Estimation change?
<--- Score

98. What is your organizations process which leads to recognition of value generation?
<--- Score

99. How is Work Planning and Estimation data gathered?
<--- Score

100. What data do you need to collect?
<--- Score

101. What qualifications and skills do you need?
<--- Score

102. Who is involved with workflow mapping?

<--- Score

103. Should you invest in industry-recognized qualifications?
<--- Score

104. Think about the functions involved in your Work Planning and Estimation project, what processes flow from these functions?
<--- Score

105. Did any value-added analysis or 'lean thinking' take place to identify some of the gaps shown on the 'as is' process map?
<--- Score

106. What data should you present in support of your report?
<--- Score

107. What methods do you use to gather Work Planning and Estimation data?
<--- Score

108. What tools were used to generate the list of possible causes?
<--- Score

109. What quality tools were used to get through the analyze phase?
<--- Score

110. What training and qualifications will you need?
<--- Score

111. What does the data say about the performance

of the stakeholder process?
<--- Score

112. What other organizational variables, such as reward systems or communication systems, affect the performance of this Work Planning and Estimation process?
<--- Score

113. How is data used for program management and improvement?
<--- Score

114. What systems/processes must you excel at?
<--- Score

115. How is the Work Planning and Estimation Value Stream Mapping managed?
<--- Score

116. What are your current levels and trends in key measures or indicators of Work Planning and Estimation product and process performance that are important to and directly serve your customers? How do these results compare with the performance of your competitors and other organizations with similar offerings?
<--- Score

117. What qualifies as competition?
<--- Score

118. What Work Planning and Estimation metrics are outputs of the process?
<--- Score

119. Does having to justify ones judgments change nature of the judgment process?
<--- Score

120. How will corresponding data be collected?
<--- Score

121. What qualifications do Work Planning and Estimation leaders need?
<--- Score

122. How was the detailed process map generated, verified, and validated?
<--- Score

123. Has an output goal been set?
<--- Score

124. Are gaps between current performance and the goal performance identified?
<--- Score

125. What are the revised rough estimates of the financial savings/opportunity for Work Planning and Estimation improvements?
<--- Score

126. What Work Planning and Estimation data will be collected?
<--- Score

127. Which Work Planning and Estimation data should be retained?
<--- Score

128. Are your outputs consistent?

<--- Score

129. How much data can be collected in the given timeframe?
<--- Score

130. What do you need to qualify?
<--- Score

131. Are you missing Work Planning and Estimation opportunities?
<--- Score

132. Do you, as a leader, bounce back quickly from setbacks?
<--- Score

Add up total points for this section:
_____ = Total points for this section

Divided by: ______ (number of statements answered) = ______
Average score for this section

Transfer your score to the Work Planning and Estimation Index at the beginning of the Self-Assessment.

CRITERION #5: IMPROVE:

INTENT: Develop a practical solution. Innovate, establish and test the solution and to measure the results.

In my belief, the answer to this question is clearly defined:

5 Strongly Agree

4 Agree

3 Neutral

2 Disagree

1 Strongly Disagree

1. Is the Work Planning and Estimation documentation thorough?
<--- Score

2. What resources are required for the improvement efforts?
<--- Score

3. What were the underlying assumptions on the cost-

benefit analysis?
<--- Score

4. Who are the Work Planning and Estimation decision makers?
<--- Score

5. How does the team improve its work?
<--- Score

6. Is a solution implementation plan established, including schedule/work breakdown structure, resources, risk management plan, cost/budget, and control plan?
<--- Score

7. Who are the people involved in developing and implementing Work Planning and Estimation?
<--- Score

8. Who will be responsible for making the decisions to include or exclude requested changes once Work Planning and Estimation is underway?
<--- Score

9. How do you measure risk?
<--- Score

10. How will you know that you have improved?
<--- Score

11. Have you identified breakpoints and/or risk tolerances that will trigger broad consideration of a potential need for intervention or modification of strategy?
<--- Score

12. How does your organization evaluate strategic Work Planning and Estimation success?
<--- Score

13. What is the risk?
<--- Score

14. Can the solution be designed and implemented within an acceptable time period?
<--- Score

15. How do you improve productivity?
<--- Score

16. Is a contingency plan established?
<--- Score

17. What risks do you need to manage?
<--- Score

18. Work Planning and Estimation risk decisions: whose call Is It?
<--- Score

19. How do you measure improved Work Planning and Estimation service perception, and satisfaction?
<--- Score

20. What criteria will you use to assess your Work Planning and Estimation risks?
<--- Score

21. How will you measure the results?
<--- Score

22. In the past few months, what is the smallest change you have made that has had the biggest positive result? What was it about that small change that produced the large return?
<--- Score

23. Is supporting Work Planning and Estimation documentation required?
<--- Score

24. How risky is your organization?
<--- Score

25. Are procedures documented for managing Work Planning and Estimation risks?
<--- Score

26. What tools were used to evaluate the potential solutions?
<--- Score

27. Were any criteria developed to assist the team in testing and evaluating potential solutions?
<--- Score

28. Is any Work Planning and Estimation documentation required?
<--- Score

29. Is there a high likelihood that any recommendations will achieve their intended results?
<--- Score

30. At what point will vulnerability assessments be performed once Work Planning and Estimation is put into production (e.g., ongoing Risk Management after

implementation)?
<--- Score

31. Was a Work Planning and Estimation charter developed?
<--- Score

32. How are policy decisions made and where?
<--- Score

33. What error proofing will be done to address some of the discrepancies observed in the 'as is' process?
<--- Score

34. Risk Identification: What are the possible risk events your organization faces in relation to Work Planning and Estimation?
<--- Score

35. Is the solution technically practical?
<--- Score

36. Is the measure of success for Work Planning and Estimation understandable to a variety of people?
<--- Score

37. Are risk triggers captured?
<--- Score

38. What is the magnitude of the improvements?
<--- Score

39. What tools were used to tap into the creativity and encourage 'outside the box' thinking?
<--- Score

40. What is the implementation plan?
<--- Score

41. How do you manage Work Planning and Estimation risk?
<--- Score

42. Explorations of the frontiers of Work Planning and Estimation will help you build influence, improve Work Planning and Estimation, optimize decision making, and sustain change, what is your approach?
<--- Score

43. Is there any other Work Planning and Estimation solution?
<--- Score

44. Where do the Work Planning and Estimation decisions reside?
<--- Score

45. How can skill-level changes improve Work Planning and Estimation?
<--- Score

46. What went well, what should change, what can improve?
<--- Score

47. How do you keep improving Work Planning and Estimation?
<--- Score

48. How can the phases of Work Planning and Estimation development be identified?
<--- Score

49. Have you achieved Work Planning and Estimation improvements?
<--- Score

50. Are you assessing Work Planning and Estimation and risk?
<--- Score

51. What is the Work Planning and Estimation's sustainability risk?
<--- Score

52. What Work Planning and Estimation improvements can be made?
<--- Score

53. What alternative responses are available to manage risk?
<--- Score

54. What strategies for Work Planning and Estimation improvement are successful?
<--- Score

55. What attendant changes will need to be made to ensure that the solution is successful?
<--- Score

56. Which of the recognised risks out of all risks can be most likely transferred?
<--- Score

57. Who will be responsible for documenting the Work Planning and Estimation requirements in detail?
<--- Score

58. What is Work Planning and Estimation's impact on utilizing the best solution(s)?
<--- Score

59. Risk events: what are the things that could go wrong?
<--- Score

60. Are risk management tasks balanced centrally and locally?
<--- Score

61. How scalable is your Work Planning and Estimation solution?
<--- Score

62. Who manages Work Planning and Estimation risk?
<--- Score

63. How will you know that a change is an improvement?
<--- Score

64. How will you recognize and celebrate results?
<--- Score

65. What is Work Planning and Estimation risk?
<--- Score

66. What does the 'should be' process map/design look like?
<--- Score

67. How do you improve Work Planning and Estimation service perception, and satisfaction?

<--- Score

68. How do you manage and improve your Work Planning and Estimation work systems to deliver customer value and achieve organizational success and sustainability?
<--- Score

69. Is pilot data collected and analyzed?
<--- Score

70. What actually has to improve and by how much?
<--- Score

71. What current systems have to be understood and/or changed?
<--- Score

72. What were the criteria for evaluating a Work Planning and Estimation pilot?
<--- Score

73. Is the Work Planning and Estimation risk managed?
<--- Score

74. How is knowledge sharing about risk management improved?
<--- Score

75. Is the optimal solution selected based on testing and analysis?
<--- Score

76. How can you better manage risk?
<--- Score

77. What are the implications of the one critical Work Planning and Estimation decision 10 minutes, 10 months, and 10 years from now?
<--- Score

78. Are decisions made in a timely manner?
<--- Score

79. Do you have the optimal project management team structure?
<--- Score

80. Who are the Work Planning and Estimation decision-makers?
<--- Score

81. Is the implementation plan designed?
<--- Score

82. Is there a small-scale pilot for proposed improvement(s)? What conclusions were drawn from the outcomes of a pilot?
<--- Score

83. To what extent does management recognize Work Planning and Estimation as a tool to increase the results?
<--- Score

84. Will the controls trigger any other risks?
<--- Score

85. Is there a cost/benefit analysis of optimal solution(s)?
<--- Score

86. Who will be using the results of the measurement activities?
<--- Score

87. What communications are necessary to support the implementation of the solution?
<--- Score

88. Does a good decision guarantee a good outcome?
<--- Score

89. When you map the key players in your own work and the types/domains of relationships with them, which relationships do you find easy and which challenging, and why?
<--- Score

90. What are the Work Planning and Estimation security risks?
<--- Score

91. What lessons, if any, from a pilot were incorporated into the design of the full-scale solution?
<--- Score

92. Does the goal represent a desired result that can be measured?
<--- Score

93. Who do you report Work Planning and Estimation results to?
<--- Score

94. What area needs the greatest improvement?
<--- Score

95. What are the affordable Work Planning and Estimation risks?
<--- Score

96. Are software development activities independent?
<--- Score

97. How do you mitigate Work Planning and Estimation risk?
<--- Score

98. How do you define the solutions' scope?
<--- Score

99. What to do with the results or outcomes of measurements?
<--- Score

100. Do you need to do a usability evaluation?
<--- Score

101. Who controls key decisions that will be made?
<--- Score

102. Are the risks fully understood, reasonable and manageable?
<--- Score

103. Is Work Planning and Estimation documentation maintained?
<--- Score

104. Are the most efficient solutions problem-specific?
<--- Score

105. Risk factors: what are the characteristics of Work Planning and Estimation that make it risky?
<--- Score

106. Is the Work Planning and Estimation solution sustainable?
<--- Score

107. How do you improve your likelihood of success ?
<--- Score

108. Is risk periodically assessed?
<--- Score

109. How can you improve performance?
<--- Score

110. How is effort estimated in agile software development projects?
<--- Score

111. What do you want to improve?
<--- Score

112. Was a pilot designed for the proposed solution(s)?
<--- Score

113. What should a proof of concept or pilot accomplish?
<--- Score

114. Do the viable solutions scale to future needs?
<--- Score

115. Can you identify any significant risks or exposures to Work Planning and Estimation third- parties (vendors, service providers, alliance partners etc) that concern you?
<--- Score

116. Do vendor agreements bring new compliance risk ?
<--- Score

117. What are the expected Work Planning and Estimation results?
<--- Score

118. What assumptions are made about the solution and approach?
<--- Score

119. What tools were most useful during the improve phase?
<--- Score

120. What are your current levels and trends in key measures or indicators of workforce and leader development?
<--- Score

121. What practices helps your organization to develop its capacity to recognize patterns?
<--- Score

122. How do the Work Planning and Estimation results compare with the performance of your competitors and other organizations with similar offerings?
<--- Score

123. Would you develop a Work Planning and Estimation Communication Strategy?
<--- Score

124. How are Work Planning and Estimation risks managed?
<--- Score

125. Do you combine technical expertise with business knowledge and Work Planning and Estimation Key topics include lifecycles, development approaches, requirements and how to make a business case?
<--- Score

126. How do you link measurement and risk?
<--- Score

127. Have milestone descriptions been developed for each milestone associated with the project?
<--- Score

128. How is continuous improvement applied to risk management?
<--- Score

129. How do you deal with Work Planning and Estimation risk?
<--- Score

130. Will you still have some results next week?
<--- Score

131. Do those selected for the Work Planning and Estimation team have a good general understanding of what Work Planning and Estimation is all about?

<--- Score

132. Are the key business and technology risks being managed?
<--- Score

133. Who makes the Work Planning and Estimation decisions in your organization?
<--- Score

134. What is the team's contingency plan for potential problems occurring in implementation?
<--- Score

135. Who should make the Work Planning and Estimation decisions?
<--- Score

136. For estimation problems, how do you develop an estimation statement?
<--- Score

137. If you could go back in time five years, what decision would you make differently? What is your best guess as to what decision you're making today you might regret five years from now?
<--- Score

138. Is the scope clearly documented?
<--- Score

139. Who manages supplier risk management in your organization?
<--- Score

140. Can you integrate quality management and risk

management?
<--- Score

141. How can you improve Work Planning and Estimation?
<--- Score

Add up total points for this section:
_____ = Total points for this section

Divided by: ______ (number of statements answered) = ______ Average score for this section

Transfer your score to the Work Planning and Estimation Index at the beginning of the Self-Assessment.

CRITERION #6: CONTROL:

INTENT: Implement the practical solution. Maintain the performance and correct possible complications.

In my belief, the answer to this question is clearly defined:

5 Strongly Agree

4 Agree

3 Neutral

2 Disagree

1 Strongly Disagree

1. Do you monitor the effectiveness of your Work Planning and Estimation activities?
<--- Score

2. Has the improved process and its steps been standardized?
<--- Score

3. Who controls critical resources?

<--- Score

4. Can support from partners be adjusted?
<--- Score

5. What Work Planning and Estimation standards are applicable?
<--- Score

6. Are there other reasons you can think of why agile estimating and planning succeed?
<--- Score

7. How estimation fits into iteration plan?
<--- Score

8. What are the duties of a planner?
<--- Score

9. Does a troubleshooting guide exist or is it needed?
<--- Score

10. Have delegated limits for deviations from plans been set?
<--- Score

11. How will the process owner verify improvement in present and future sigma levels, process capabilities?
<--- Score

12. Will your goals reflect your program budget?
<--- Score

13. Who is the Work Planning and Estimation process owner?
<--- Score

14. Is it clear what is within the scope of the piece of work you are planning?
<--- Score

15. What is going according to plan?
<--- Score

16. Are you clear about the purpose of the plan?
<--- Score

17. What quality tools were useful in the control phase?
<--- Score

18. Is new knowledge gained imbedded in the response plan?
<--- Score

19. Does job training on the documented procedures need to be part of the process team's education and training?
<--- Score

20. Have all resource owners committed to the plan?
<--- Score

21. What is the right amount of planning on your current project?
<--- Score

22. Is there a transfer of ownership and knowledge to process owner and process team tasked with the responsibilities.
<--- Score

23. What is the best design framework for Work Planning and Estimation organization now that, in a post industrial-age if the top-down, command and control model is no longer relevant?
<--- Score

24. What is the standard deviation of the activity equal?
<--- Score

25. What does an agile project plan look like?
<--- Score

26. Will the team be available to assist members in planning investigations?
<--- Score

27. How will the process owner and team be able to hold the gains?
<--- Score

28. Are operating procedures consistent?
<--- Score

29. Which of the dozen guidelines apply to your current estimation and planning process?
<--- Score

30. Do you monitor the Work Planning and Estimation decisions made and fine tune them as they evolve?
<--- Score

31. What is the standard for acceptable Work Planning and Estimation performance?
<--- Score

32. Do the Work Planning and Estimation decisions you make today help people and the planet tomorrow?
<--- Score

33. How do you start planning without any information on hand?
<--- Score

34. Is a response plan in place for when the input, process, or output measures indicate an 'out-of-control' condition?
<--- Score

35. Have new or revised work instructions resulted?
<--- Score

36. What are the known security controls?
<--- Score

37. Does the plan identify formal quality controls and audit activities?
<--- Score

38. How will report readings be checked to effectively monitor performance?
<--- Score

39. Does the response plan contain a definite closed loop continual improvement scheme (e.g., plan-do-check-act)?
<--- Score

40. How do you monitor usage and cost?
<--- Score

41. How widespread is its use?
<--- Score

42. Which approach to iteration planning do you prefer, velocity driven or commitment driven?
<--- Score

43. What is needed for a successful project plan?
<--- Score

44. Is your current project buffered against any types of uncertainty?
<--- Score

45. How will Work Planning and Estimation decisions be made and monitored?
<--- Score

46. Against what alternative is success being measured?
<--- Score

47. How do you spread information?
<--- Score

48. Are there documented procedures?
<--- Score

49. What does a project management plan include?
<--- Score

50. Who will be in control?
<--- Score

51. Are the planned controls working?
<--- Score

52. Does the Work Planning and Estimation performance meet the customer's requirements?
<--- Score

53. How will the day-to-day responsibilities for monitoring and continual improvement be transferred from the improvement team to the process owner?
<--- Score

54. What other systems, operations, processes, and infrastructures (hiring practices, staffing, training, incentives/rewards, metrics/dashboards/scorecards, etc.) need updates, additions, changes, or deletions in order to facilitate knowledge transfer and improvements?
<--- Score

55. How will new or emerging customer needs/requirements be checked/communicated to orient the process toward meeting the new specifications and continually reducing variation?
<--- Score

56. Is a response plan established and deployed?
<--- Score

57. Have you adjusted the timing and allocation of work to spread the load evenly?
<--- Score

58. Have lessons learned been recorded and disseminated to interested parties?

<--- Score

59. How will input, process, and output variables be checked to detect for sub-optimal conditions?
<--- Score

60. What are you attempting to measure/monitor?
<--- Score

61. How it fits into iteration plan?
<--- Score

62. What are customers monitoring?
<--- Score

63. Is there a documented and implemented monitoring plan?
<--- Score

64. Is there a control plan in place for sustaining improvements (short and long-term)?
<--- Score

65. What is your theory of human motivation, and how does your compensation plan fit with that view?
<--- Score

66. What is velocity and how do you use it for planning & refining estimates?
<--- Score

67. How is change control managed?
<--- Score

68. In the case of a Work Planning and Estimation project, the criteria for the audit derive from

implementation objectives, an audit of a Work Planning and Estimation project involves assessing whether the recommendations outlined for implementation have been met, can you track that any Work Planning and Estimation project is implemented as planned, and is it working?
<--- Score

69. How do senior leaders actions reflect a commitment to the organizations Work Planning and Estimation values?
<--- Score

70. What is the recommended frequency of auditing?
<--- Score

71. What are the key elements of your Work Planning and Estimation performance improvement system, including your evaluation, organizational learning, and innovation processes?
<--- Score

72. Can the project be constructed as planned?
<--- Score

73. Are controls in place and consistently applied?
<--- Score

74. Are suggested corrective/restorative actions indicated on the response plan for known causes to problems that might surface?
<--- Score

75. Is there a standardized process?
<--- Score

76. Is there documentation that will support the successful operation of the improvement?
<--- Score

77. Are the Work Planning and Estimation standards challenging?
<--- Score

78. Does Work Planning and Estimation appropriately measure and monitor risk?
<--- Score

79. Is there an action plan in case of emergencies?
<--- Score

80. What other areas of the group might benefit from the Work Planning and Estimation team's improvements, knowledge, and learning?
<--- Score

81. Who has control over resources?
<--- Score

82. Is reporting being used or needed?
<--- Score

83. How is Work Planning and Estimation project cost planned, managed, monitored?
<--- Score

84. What should the next improvement project be that is related to Work Planning and Estimation?
<--- Score

85. Where do ideas that reach policy makers and planners as proposals for Work Planning and

Estimation strengthening and reform actually originate?
<--- Score

86. Do you need to plan what will be worked on in each iteration?
<--- Score

87. Are documented procedures clear and easy to follow for the operators?
<--- Score

88. Is the Work Planning and Estimation test/ monitoring cost justified?
<--- Score

89. Do you understand the objectives to be met by the plan?
<--- Score

90. How do your controls stack up?
<--- Score

91. What is the best software for planning?
<--- Score

92. Are there any assumptions you must make in order to construct the plan?
<--- Score

93. Are new process steps, standards, and documentation ingrained into normal operations?
<--- Score

94. What should you measure to verify efficiency gains?

<--- Score

95. Implementation Planning: is a pilot needed to test the changes before a full roll out occurs?
<--- Score

96. How might the group capture best practices and lessons learned so as to leverage improvements?
<--- Score

97. What is the control/monitoring plan?
<--- Score

98. What do you measure to verify effectiveness gains?
<--- Score

99. What is project management plan?
<--- Score

100. Who is going to spread your message?
<--- Score

101. How useful are the particular agile effort estimation methods in the agile planning process?
<--- Score

102. What is the difference between recovery plan and revised plan?
<--- Score

103. Is the project planned to occur in the short term?
<--- Score

104. What are the critical parameters to watch?

<--- Score

105. Can you adapt and adjust to changing Work Planning and Estimation situations?
<--- Score

106. Has the Work Planning and Estimation value of standards been quantified?
<--- Score

107. What are your results for key measures or indicators of the accomplishment of your Work Planning and Estimation strategy and action plans, including building and strengthening core competencies?
<--- Score

108. How do you select, collect, align, and integrate Work Planning and Estimation data and information for tracking daily operations and overall organizational performance, including progress relative to strategic objectives and action plans?
<--- Score

109. How do you encourage people to take control and responsibility?
<--- Score

110. How do you establish and deploy modified action plans if circumstances require a shift in plans and rapid execution of new plans?
<--- Score

111. What can you control?
<--- Score

112. Is knowledge gained on process shared and institutionalized?
<--- Score

113. What is the best way to be professional planning engineer?
<--- Score

114. Will any special training be provided for results interpretation?
<--- Score

115. Are the planned controls in place?
<--- Score

116. What key inputs and outputs are being measured on an ongoing basis?
<--- Score

117. Is there a recommended audit plan for routine surveillance inspections of Work Planning and Estimation's gains?
<--- Score

118. Is there a Work Planning and Estimation Communication plan covering who needs to get what information when?
<--- Score

119. Is there a plan for a post implementation review of benefits?
<--- Score

120. How likely is the current Work Planning and Estimation plan to come in on schedule or on budget?
<--- Score

Add up total points for this section:
_____ = Total points for this section

Divided by: ______ (number of statements answered) = ______
Average score for this section

Transfer your score to the Work Planning and Estimation Index at the beginning of the Self-Assessment.

CRITERION #7: SUSTAIN:

INTENT: Retain the benefits.

In my belief, the answer to this question is clearly defined:

5 Strongly Agree

4 Agree

3 Neutral

2 Disagree

1 Strongly Disagree

1. Do you meet your time constraints/target delivery dates?
<--- Score

2. What are the business goals Work Planning and Estimation is aiming to achieve?
<--- Score

3. In retrospect, of the projects that you pulled the plug on, what percent do you wish had been allowed to keep going, and what percent do you wish had

ended earlier?
<--- Score

4. Where the activity should be performed?
<--- Score

5. What role does communication play in the success or failure of a Work Planning and Estimation project?
<--- Score

6. How do you estimate activities durations?
<--- Score

7. Which artifacts helps to bring product owner and team together collaboratively?
<--- Score

8. If no one would ever find out about your accomplishments, how would you lead differently?
<--- Score

9. What was the last experiment you ran?
<--- Score

10. At what moment would you think; Will I get fired?
<--- Score

11. What projects are going on in the organization today, and what resources are those projects using from the resource pools?
<--- Score

12. How should a team count a partially finished story when determining velocity?
<--- Score

13. What new services of functionality will be implemented next with Work Planning and Estimation ?
<--- Score

14. How do you assess the Work Planning and Estimation pitfalls that are inherent in implementing it?
<--- Score

15. If you weren't already in this business, would you enter it today? And if not, what are you going to do about it?
<--- Score

16. What have you done to protect your business from competitive encroachment?
<--- Score

17. How do you keep records, of what?
<--- Score

18. What is your BATNA (best alternative to a negotiated agreement)?
<--- Score

19. How do you foster the skills, knowledge, talents, attributes, and characteristics you want to have?
<--- Score

20. Which approach do you prefer story points or ideal days?
<--- Score

21. Is there any reason to believe the opposite of my current belief?

<--- Score

22. What business benefits will Work Planning and Estimation goals deliver if achieved?
<--- Score

23. Will there be any necessary staff changes (redundancies or new hires)?
<--- Score

24. If you find that you havent accomplished one of the goals for one of the steps of the Work Planning and Estimation strategy, what will you do to fix it?
<--- Score

25. How do you determine the key elements that affect Work Planning and Estimation workforce satisfaction, how are these elements determined for different workforce groups and segments?
<--- Score

26. How will you make a manpower loading for your schedule?
<--- Score

27. Are assumptions made in Work Planning and Estimation stated explicitly?
<--- Score

28. Which represents the richest and most effective mode of communication in a team?
<--- Score

29. What are the challenges?
<--- Score

30. Who are the key stakeholders?
<--- Score

31. What is the purpose of Work Planning and Estimation in relation to the mission?
<--- Score

32. How do you provide a safe environment -physically and emotionally?
<--- Score

33. Is it clear which aspects of the project are of most interest to a particular stakeholder?
<--- Score

34. How do you listen to customers to obtain actionable information?
<--- Score

35. How do you deal with Work Planning and Estimation changes?
<--- Score

36. What is the estimated value of the project?
<--- Score

37. Do you see more potential in people than they do in themselves?
<--- Score

38. How significant are team interdependencies on your project?
<--- Score

39. Marketing budgets are tighter, consumers are more skeptical, and social media has changed forever

the way we talk about Work Planning and Estimation, how do you gain traction?
<--- Score

40. To whom do you add value?
<--- Score

41. What counts that you are not counting?
<--- Score

42. Were lessons learned captured and communicated?
<--- Score

43. Is a particular feature worth delaying the release?
<--- Score

44. What work will be included in the project?
<--- Score

45. What do we do when new problems arise?
<--- Score

46. Have benefits been optimized with all key stakeholders?
<--- Score

47. Are you satisfied with your current role? If not, what is missing from it?
<--- Score

48. If you were responsible for initiating and implementing major changes in your organization, what steps might you take to ensure acceptance of those changes?

<--- Score

49. What stupid rule would you most like to kill?
<--- Score

50. Which project should be terminated first?
<--- Score

51. What happens if you do not have enough funding?
<--- Score

52. Do you have the right people on the bus?
<--- Score

53. How many points should the team count toward the velocity of the current iteration?
<--- Score

54. What is it like to work for you?
<--- Score

55. Who is the main stakeholder, with ultimate responsibility for driving Work Planning and Estimation forward?
<--- Score

56. What unique value proposition (UVP) do you offer?
<--- Score

57. Who are your customers?
<--- Score

58. Why do and why don't your customers like your organization?
<--- Score

59. Who will provide the final approval of Work Planning and Estimation deliverables?
<--- Score

60. Do you think Work Planning and Estimation accomplishes the goals you expect it to accomplish?
<--- Score

61. What are the short and long-term Work Planning and Estimation goals?
<--- Score

62. Who uses your product in ways you never expected?
<--- Score

63. How do you make it meaningful in connecting Work Planning and Estimation with what users do day-to-day?
<--- Score

64. Do you have enough freaky customers in your portfolio pushing you to the limit day in and day out?
<--- Score

65. Are projects different from the other work?
<--- Score

66. Who are four people whose careers you have enhanced?
<--- Score

67. What are the gaps in your knowledge and experience?
<--- Score

68. What goals did you miss?
<--- Score

69. What potential megatrends could make your business model obsolete?
<--- Score

70. In the past year, what have you done (or could you have done) to increase the accurate perception of your company/brand as ethical and honest?
<--- Score

71. Which are valid project selection methods?
<--- Score

72. What is your formula for success in Work Planning and Estimation ?
<--- Score

73. Who, on the executive team or the board, has spoken to a customer recently?
<--- Score

74. How do customers see your organization?
<--- Score

75. What are the barriers to increased Work Planning and Estimation production?
<--- Score

76. Who is responsible for ensuring appropriate resources (time, people and money) are allocated to Work Planning and Estimation?
<--- Score

77. What should the team members be thinking of now?
<--- Score

78. How do you maintain Work Planning and Estimation's Integrity?
<--- Score

79. How can you become more high-tech but still be high touch?
<--- Score

80. Are you maintaining a past–present–future perspective throughout the Work Planning and Estimation discussion?
<--- Score

81. How can you negotiate Work Planning and Estimation successfully with a stubborn boss, an irate client, or a deceitful coworker?
<--- Score

82. What are the potential basics of Work Planning and Estimation fraud?
<--- Score

83. When information truly is ubiquitous, when reach and connectivity are completely global, when computing resources are infinite, and when a whole new set of impossibilities are not only possible, but happening, what will that do to your business?
<--- Score

84. What are the long-term Work Planning and Estimation goals?
<--- Score

85. What is the choice that the team makes?
<--- Score

86. How do you decide how much to remunerate an employee?
<--- Score

87. What must you excel at?
<--- Score

88. Whose voice (department, ethnic group, women, older workers, etc) might you have missed hearing from in your company, and how might you amplify this voice to create positive momentum for your business?
<--- Score

89. How do you go about securing Work Planning and Estimation?
<--- Score

90. How do you ensure that implementations of Work Planning and Estimation products are done in a way that ensures safety?
<--- Score

91. How is implementation research currently incorporated into each of your goals?
<--- Score

92. Would you rather sell to knowledgeable and informed customers or to uninformed customers?
<--- Score

93. How are you doing compared to your industry?

<--- Score

94. How would working as a unified whole team have affected your current or last project?
<--- Score

95. What is an unauthorized commitment?
<--- Score

96. Can the schedule be done in the given time?
<--- Score

97. Is there a work around that you can use?
<--- Score

98. What is the big Work Planning and Estimation idea?
<--- Score

99. What are the conditions of satisfaction on your current project?
<--- Score

100. If your company went out of business tomorrow, would anyone who doesn't get a paycheck here care?
<--- Score

101. How do you manage Work Planning and Estimation Knowledge Management (KM)?
<--- Score

102. Is a Work Planning and Estimation breakthrough on the horizon?
<--- Score

103. What are the things the team should do now?

<--- Score

104. How can you become the company that would put you out of business?
<--- Score

105. How would you model the return for a theme on your current project?
<--- Score

106. What are the top 3 things at the forefront of your Work Planning and Estimation agendas for the next 3 years?
<--- Score

107. Are the assumptions believable and achievable?
<--- Score

108. Is Work Planning and Estimation dependent on the successful delivery of a current project?
<--- Score

109. What might you try to increase the amount of time each person is able to devote to the project?
<--- Score

110. Do you say no to customers for no reason?
<--- Score

111. Did you have a hard time making up your mind?
<--- Score

112. Are all key stakeholders present at all Structured Walkthroughs?
<--- Score

113. Do you feel that more should be done in the Work Planning and Estimation area?
<--- Score

114. Whom among your colleagues do you trust, and for what?
<--- Score

115. What are you challenging?
<--- Score

116. What are your most important goals for the strategic Work Planning and Estimation objectives?
<--- Score

117. Who is on the team?
<--- Score

118. What is the key benefit that the customer will get by using the product?
<--- Score

119. If there were zero limitations, what would you do differently?
<--- Score

120. Why is it important to have senior management support for a Work Planning and Estimation project?
<--- Score

121. Do you know who is a friend or a foe?
<--- Score

122. How do you cross-sell and up-sell your Work Planning and Estimation success?

<--- Score

123. Is maximizing Work Planning and Estimation protection the same as minimizing Work Planning and Estimation loss?
<--- Score

124. Why is Work Planning and Estimation important for you now?
<--- Score

125. HoW should each activity be performed?
<--- Score

126. How will you insure seamless interoperability of Work Planning and Estimation moving forward?
<--- Score

127. What is the work to be estimated?
<--- Score

128. Will there be a change to the timing of delivery of any benefits?
<--- Score

129. What are you trying to prove to yourself, and how might it be hijacking your life and business success?
<--- Score

130. Who do you think the world wants your organization to be?
<--- Score

131. How do you accomplish your long range Work Planning and Estimation goals?
<--- Score

132. Is a Work Planning and Estimation team work effort in place?
<--- Score

133. Who is responsible for Work Planning and Estimation?
<--- Score

134. What are the key enablers to make this Work Planning and Estimation move?
<--- Score

135. How can you incorporate support to ensure safe and effective use of Work Planning and Estimation into the services that you provide?
<--- Score

136. What is the overall talent health of your organization as a whole at senior levels, and for each organization reporting to a member of the Senior Leadership Team?
<--- Score

137. Who is responsible for errors?
<--- Score

138. Is the impact that Work Planning and Estimation has shown?
<--- Score

139. How do you set Work Planning and Estimation stretch targets and how do you get people to not only participate in setting these stretch targets but also that they strive to achieve these?
<--- Score

140. How do you foster innovation?
<--- Score

141. What is the hourly rate of pay for each person on the project?
<--- Score

142. What could happen if you do not do it?
<--- Score

143. In a project to restructure Work Planning and Estimation outcomes, which stakeholders would you involve?
<--- Score

144. Are you relevant? Will you be relevant five years from now? Ten?
<--- Score

145. What will be the consequences to the stakeholder (financial, reputation etc) if Work Planning and Estimation does not go ahead or fails to deliver the objectives?
<--- Score

146. Who in the project will be responsible for escalation?
<--- Score

147. Are you still looking at the same schedule?
<--- Score

148. Are the criteria for selecting recommendations stated?
<--- Score

149. How do you lead with Work Planning and Estimation in mind?
<--- Score

150. What management system can you use to leverage the Work Planning and Estimation experience, ideas, and concerns of the people closest to the work to be done?
<--- Score

151. How will you motivate the stakeholders with the least vested interest?
<--- Score

152. Who should perform the activity?
<--- Score

153. Think of your Work Planning and Estimation project, what are the main functions?
<--- Score

154. Which is the least recommended way to determine the initial velocity of a team?
<--- Score

155. What is the most important thing that your organization should do?
<--- Score

156. Can you do all this work?
<--- Score

157. What is the appropriate iteration for your current project?
<--- Score

158. Which models, tools and techniques are necessary?
<--- Score

159. What is the interest in the project?
<--- Score

160. What is the way to resolve the delay in project time?
<--- Score

161. What is the kind of project structure that would be appropriate for your Work Planning and Estimation project, should it be formal and complex, or can it be less formal and relatively simple?
<--- Score

162. Who do you want your customers to become?
<--- Score

163. Does the tool support the estimation of maintenance & enhancement projects?
<--- Score

164. Which individuals, teams or departments will be involved in Work Planning and Estimation?
<--- Score

165. Does the project involve complex staging of works?
<--- Score

166. What is the craziest thing you can do?
<--- Score

167. How much contingency will be available in the budget?
<--- Score

168. Is your basic point ______ or ______?
<--- Score

169. What are the options available to the team?
<--- Score

170. What types of benefits are anticipated?
<--- Score

171. How important is Work Planning and Estimation to the user organizations mission?
<--- Score

172. What is something you believe that nearly no one agrees with you on?
<--- Score

173. How do senior leaders deploy your organizations vision and values through your leadership system, to the workforce, to key suppliers and partners, and to customers and other stakeholders, as appropriate?
<--- Score

174. When should the activity be performed?
<--- Score

175. What is the reasonable range of float you assume while checking the look ahead work activities?
<--- Score

176. What is thresholds in project management?

<--- Score

177. What are current Work Planning and Estimation paradigms?
<--- Score

178. Is it economical; do you have the time and money?
<--- Score

179. When should you bother with diagrams?
<--- Score

180. Is Work Planning and Estimation realistic, or are you setting yourself up for failure?
<--- Score

181. Will any individuals or skill/types be overloaded with project work at any time?
<--- Score

182. What activities have to be performed?
<--- Score

183. Is there any way to get an expected schedule now?
<--- Score

184. How do you transition from the baseline to the target?
<--- Score

185. Operational - will it work?
<--- Score

186. What happens when a new employee joins the

organization?
<--- Score

187. Have new benefits been realized?
<--- Score

188. Why should you adopt a Work Planning and Estimation framework?
<--- Score

189. Why not do Work Planning and Estimation?
<--- Score

190. What happens at your organization when people fail?
<--- Score

191. What would have to be true for the option on the table to be the best possible choice?
<--- Score

192. How do you get information to populate and update your schedule?
<--- Score

193. What should the team member do first?
<--- Score

194. What is the overall business strategy?
<--- Score

195. What will the benefits be to external stakeholders?
<--- Score

196. How will you know that the Work Planning and

Estimation project has been successful?
<--- Score

197. What information is critical to your organization that your executives are ignoring?
<--- Score

198. What is your Work Planning and Estimation strategy?
<--- Score

199. What knowledge, skills and characteristics mark a good Work Planning and Estimation project manager?
<--- Score

200. What trouble can you get into?
<--- Score

201. Is a schedule included with the estimate?
<--- Score

202. Political -is anyone trying to undermine this project?
<--- Score

203. Which is going to be least effective in increasing velocity of the team?
<--- Score

204. When will the work be accomplished?
<--- Score

205. Are new benefits received and understood?
<--- Score

206. Why will customers want to buy your

organizations products/services?
<--- Score

207. How likely is it that a customer would recommend your company to a friend or colleague?
<--- Score

208. Did your employees make progress today?
<--- Score

209. Ask yourself: how would you do this work if you only had one staff member to do it?
<--- Score

210. Are there any activities that you can take off your to do list?
<--- Score

211. What does your signature ensure?
<--- Score

212. How long will the project team take to complete the project?
<--- Score

213. How do you proactively clarify deliverables and Work Planning and Estimation quality expectations?
<--- Score

214. How do you create buy-in?
<--- Score

215. What are specific Work Planning and Estimation rules to follow?
<--- Score

216. What is effective Work Planning and Estimation?
<--- Score

217. What you are going to do to affect the numbers?
<--- Score

218. What threat is Work Planning and Estimation addressing?
<--- Score

219. How does Work Planning and Estimation integrate with other stakeholder initiatives?
<--- Score

220. Who have you, as a company, historically been when you've been at your best?
<--- Score

221. Who do we want your customers to become?
<--- Score

222. Are you ahead or behind schedule?
<--- Score

223. Can you break it down?
<--- Score

224. What are the essentials of internal Work Planning and Estimation management?
<--- Score

225. What is the difference between recovery schedule and revised schedule?
<--- Score

226. Has implementation been effective in reaching

specified objectives so far?
<--- Score

227. If your customer were your grandmother, would you tell her to buy what you're selling?
<--- Score

228. How long will it take to change?
<--- Score

229. Which is a correct pairing of adaptive leadership and team phases?
<--- Score

230. What is the normal total float allowed for a new project?
<--- Score

231. How long will the project take if you add the characters?
<--- Score

232. Do you have past Work Planning and Estimation successes?
<--- Score

233. What is the likely productivity of the team per team size?
<--- Score

234. Is there a loss or other significant change in potential benefits?
<--- Score

235. Do you think you know, or do you know you know ?

<--- Score

236. Has the project delivery / procurement method been determined?
<--- Score

237. Is the Work Planning and Estimation organization completing tasks effectively and efficiently?
<--- Score

Add up total points for this section:
_____ = Total points for this section

Divided by: ______ (number of statements answered) = ______
Average score for this section

Transfer your score to the Work Planning and Estimation Index at the beginning of the Self-Assessment.

Work Planning And Estimation and Managing Projects, Criteria for Project Managers:

1.0 Initiating Process Group: Work Planning And Estimation

1. Information sharing?

2. Are the changes in your Work Planning And Estimation project being formally requested, analyzed, and approved by the appropriate decision makers?

3. The Work Planning And Estimation project managers have maximum authority in which type of organization?

4. During which stage of Risk planning are risks prioritized based on probability and impact?

5. Just how important is your work to the overall success of the Work Planning And Estimation project?

6. Who is involved in each phase?

7. Based on your Work Planning And Estimation project communication management plan, what worked well?

8. Establishment of pm office?

9. Mitigate. what will you do to minimize the impact should the risk event occur?

10. What were things that you did very well and want to do the same again on the next Work Planning And Estimation project?

11. What communication items need improvement?

12. How do you help others satisfy needs?

13. What were the challenges that you encountered during the execution of a previous Work Planning And Estimation project that you would not want to repeat?

14. How should needs be met?

15. How well did you do?

16. Are you certain deliverables are properly completed and meet quality standards?

17. Who does what?

18. Were escalated issues resolved promptly?

19. What will you do?

20. What were things that you did well, and could improve, and how?

1.1 Project Charter: Work Planning And Estimation

21. Customer: who are you doing the Work Planning And Estimation project for?

22. Is it an improvement over existing products?

23. Assumptions and constraints: what assumptions were made in defining the Work Planning And Estimation project?

24. What outcome, in measureable terms, are you hoping to accomplish?

25. What material?

26. Why Outsource?

27. What metrics could you look at?

28. What is the purpose of the Work Planning And Estimation project?

29. Work Planning And Estimation project background: what is the primary motivation for this Work Planning And Estimation project?

30. Why is it important?

31. Work Planning And Estimation project deliverables: what is the Work Planning And Estimation project going to produce?

32. Who are the stakeholders?

33. Did your Work Planning And Estimation project ask for this?

34. What is the business need?

35. Are you building in-house ?

36. Why do you need to manage scope?

37. Major high-level milestone targets: what events measure progress?

38. What are the constraints?

39. What changes can you make to improve?

40. Must Have?

1.2 Stakeholder Register: Work Planning And Estimation

41. How should employers make voices heard?

42. How will reports be created?

43. How much influence do they have on the Work Planning And Estimation project?

44. What are the major Work Planning And Estimation project milestones requiring communications or providing communications opportunities?

45. What opportunities exist to provide communications?

46. What & Why?

47. Is your organization ready for change?

48. What is the power of the stakeholder?

49. Who is managing stakeholder engagement?

50. How big is the gap?

51. Who wants to talk about Security?

1.3 Stakeholder Analysis Matrix: Work Planning And Estimation

52. New USPs?

53. What is the range you need to look at?

54. Experience, knowledge, data?

55. Market developments?

56. How do customers express needs?

57. Are the required specifications for products or services changing?

58. Who are potential allies and opponents?

59. What is your organizations competitors doing?

60. What are the reimbursement requirements?

61. Price, value, quality?

62. What is the stakeholders name, what is function?

63. What tools would help you communicate?

64. Marketing - reach, distribution, awareness?

65. Business and product development?

66. Who is most interested in information about the

topic and/or has previously initiated interest?

67. Where are mitigation costs factored in?

68. What advantages do your organizations stakeholders have?

69. How much do resources cost?

70. Do recommendations include actions to address any differential distribution of impacts?

71. What is relationship with the Work Planning And Estimation project?

2.0 Planning Process Group: Work Planning And Estimation

72. How do you integrate Work Planning And Estimation project Planning with the Iterative/ Evolutionary SDLC?

73. In which Work Planning And Estimation project management process group is the detailed Work Planning And Estimation project budget created?

74. What do you need to do?

75. Is your organization showing technical capacity and leadership commitment to keep working with the Work Planning And Estimation project and to repeat it?

76. How will it affect you?

77. To what extent are the participating departments coordinating with each other?

78. In what way has the program contributed towards the issue culture and development included on the public agenda?

79. Will you be replaced?

80. Did the program design/ implementation strategy adequately address the planning stage necessary to set up structures, hire staff etc.?

81. Why do it Work Planning And Estimation projects fail?

82. Why is it important to determine activity sequencing on Work Planning And Estimation projects?

83. Are the follow-up indicators relevant and do they meet the quality needed to measure the outputs and outcomes of the Work Planning And Estimation project?

84. What are the different approaches to building the WBS?

85. Does it make any difference if you are successful?

86. You did your readings, yes?

87. When developing the estimates for Work Planning And Estimation project phases, you choose to add the individual estimates for the activities that comprise each phase. What type of estimation method are you using?

88. Are there efficient coordination mechanisms to avoid overloading the counterparts, participating stakeholders?

89. What should you do next?

90. What types of differentiated effects are resulting from the Work Planning And Estimation project and to what extent?

91. Is the Work Planning And Estimation project

making progress in helping to achieve the set results?

2.1 Project Management Plan: Work Planning And Estimation

92. When is a Work Planning And Estimation project management plan created?

93. Are there any scope changes proposed for a previously authorized Work Planning And Estimation project?

94. Development trends and opportunities. What if the positive direction and vision of your organization causes expected trends to change?

95. Who manages integration?

96. What if, for example, the positive direction and vision of your organization causes expected trends to change resulting in greater need than expected?

97. Are cost risk analysis methods applied to develop contingencies for the estimated total Work Planning And Estimation project costs?

98. Will you add a schedule and diagram?

99. How can you best help your organization to develop consistent practices in Work Planning And Estimation project management planning stages?

100. Do there need to be organizational changes?

101. What does management expect of PMs?

102. Do the proposed changes from the Work Planning And Estimation project include any significant risks to safety?

103. Who is the sponsor?

104. What are the assigned resources?

105. Are there any Client staffing expectations?

106. Has the selected plan been formulated using cost effectiveness and incremental analysis techniques?

107. What went wrong?

108. If the Work Planning And Estimation project management plan is a comprehensive document that guides you in Work Planning And Estimation project execution and control, then what should it NOT contain?

109. Is mitigation authorized or recommended?

110. What are the deliverables?

2.2 Scope Management Plan: Work Planning And Estimation

111. Are there any windfall benefits that would accrue to the Work Planning And Estimation project sponsor or other parties?

112. Are non-critical path items updated and agreed upon with the teams?

113. Has the budget been baselined?

114. What is the need the Work Planning And Estimation project will address?

115. Describe the manner in which Work Planning And Estimation project deliverables will be formally presented and accepted. Will they be presented at the end of each phase?

116. Is there a set of procedures defining the scope, procedures, and deliverables defining quality control?

117. Are the payment terms being followed?

118. Has allowance been made for vacations, holidays, training (learning time for each team member), staff promotions & staff turnovers?

119. Has appropriate allowance been made for the effect of the learning curve on all personnel joining the Work Planning And Estimation project who do not have the required prior industry, functional &

technical expertise?

120. What is the estimated cost of creating and implementing?

121. Given the scope of the Work Planning And Estimation project, which criterion should be optimized?

122. Does the business case include how the Work Planning And Estimation project aligns with your organizations strategic goals & objectives?

123. Have adequate resources been provided by management to ensure Work Planning And Estimation project success?

124. Can each item be appropriately scheduled?

125. Is current scope of the Work Planning And Estimation project substantially different than that originally defined?

126. Are issues raised, assessed, actioned, and resolved in a timely and efficient manner?

127. Are written status reports provided on a designated frequent basis?

128. Is the Work Planning And Estimation project status reviewed with the steering and executive teams at appropriate intervals?

129. Are the results of quality assurance reviews provided to affected groups & individuals?

130. Materials available for performing the work?

2.3 Requirements Management Plan: Work Planning And Estimation

131. How knowledgeable is the primary Stakeholder(s) in the proposed application area?

132. How do you know that you have done this right?

133. What is a problem?

134. Should you include sub-activities?

135. Who will initially review the Work Planning And Estimation project work or products to ensure it meets the applicable acceptance criteria?

136. Did you get proper approvals?

137. Is it new or replacing an existing business system or process?

138. Has the requirements team been instructed in the Change Control process?

139. Do you have price sheets and a methodology for determining the total proposal cost?

140. Is requirements work dependent on any other specific Work Planning And Estimation project or non-Work Planning And Estimation project activities (e.g. funding, approvals, procurement)?

141. Do you know which stakeholders will participate

in the requirements effort?

142. Who will perform the analysis?

143. What performance metrics will be used?

144. How will bidders price evaluations be done, by deliverables, phases, or in a big bang?

145. Is the user satisfied?

146. What information regarding the Work Planning And Estimation project requirements will be reported?

147. Will you use an assessment of the Work Planning And Estimation project environment as a tool to discover risk to the requirements process?

148. Could inaccurate or incomplete requirements in this Work Planning And Estimation project create a serious risk for the business?

149. How often will the reporting occur?

150. When and how will a requirements baseline be established in this Work Planning And Estimation project?

2.4 Requirements Documentation: Work Planning And Estimation

151. The problem with gathering requirements is right there in the word gathering. What images does it conjure?

152. What if the system wasn t implemented?

153. Does the system provide the functions which best support the customers needs?

154. How much testing do you need to do to prove that your system is safe?

155. What are current process problems?

156. What is the risk associated with cost and schedule?

157. Where do system and software requirements come from, what are sources?

158. Who is interacting with the system?

159. Can the requirements be checked?

160. How will requirements be documented and who signs off on them?

161. Is the origin of the requirement clearly stated?

162. What is your Elevator Speech?

163. What is the risk associated with the technology?

164. Completeness. are all functions required by the customer included?

165. Where do you define what is a customer, what are the attributes of customer?

166. Validity. does the system provide the functions which best support the customers needs?

167. What can tools do for us?

168. Do technical resources exist?

169. What happens when requirements are wrong?

170. How much does requirements engineering cost?

2.5 Requirements Traceability Matrix: Work Planning And Estimation

171. Why use a WBS?

172. What percentage of Work Planning And Estimation projects are producing traceability matrices between requirements and other work products?

173. Why do you manage scope?

174. How small is small enough?

175. How do you manage scope?

176. How will it affect the stakeholders personally in career?

177. Describe the process for approving requirements so they can be added to the traceability matrix and Work Planning And Estimation project work can be performed. Will the Work Planning And Estimation project requirements become approved in writing?

178. Is there a requirements traceability process in place?

179. Do you have a clear understanding of all subcontracts in place?

180. What are the chronologies, contingencies, consequences, criteria?

181. Will you use a Requirements Traceability Matrix?

182. What is the WBS?

2.6 Project Scope Statement: Work Planning And Estimation

183. Is the Work Planning And Estimation project manager qualified and experienced in Work Planning And Estimation project management?

184. Work Planning And Estimation project lead, team lead, solution architect?

185. Were potential customers involved early in the planning process?

186. What should you drop in order to add something new?

187. Do you anticipate new stakeholders joining the Work Planning And Estimation project over time?

188. If there are vendors, have they signed off on the Work Planning And Estimation project Plan?

189. Is the quality function identified and assigned?

190. Is the plan for your organization of the Work Planning And Estimation project resources adequate?

191. Will this process be communicated to the customer and Work Planning And Estimation project team?

192. Are there specific processes you will use to evaluate and approve/reject changes?

193. Is an issue management process documented and filed?

194. Are there backup strategies for key members of the Work Planning And Estimation project?

195. Will the risk status be reported to management on a regular and frequent basis?

196. Have the reports to be produced, distributed, and filed been defined?

197. Is the scope of your Work Planning And Estimation project well defined?

198. Does the scope statement still need some clarity?

199. Is the change control process documented and on file?

200. Has a method and process for requirement tracking been developed?

2.7 Assumption and Constraint Log: Work Planning And Estimation

201. How can constraints be violated?

202. Would known impacts serve as impediments?

203. Are best practices and metrics employed to identify issues, progress, performance, etc.?

204. Have the scope, objectives, costs, benefits and impacts been communicated to all involved and/or impacted stakeholders and work groups?

205. Security analysis has access to information that is sanitized?

206. Has the approach and development strategy of the Work Planning And Estimation project been defined, documented and accepted by the appropriate stakeholders?

207. Have adequate resources been provided by management to ensure Work Planning And Estimation project success?

208. What to do at recovery?

209. Should factors be unpredictable over time?

210. Are you meeting your customers expectations consistently?

211. Diagrams and tables are included to account for complex concepts and increase overall readability?

212. Are funding and staffing resource estimates sufficiently detailed and documented for use in planning and tracking the Work Planning And Estimation project?

213. After observing execution of process, is it in compliance with the documented Plan?

214. Is staff trained on the software technologies that are being used on the Work Planning And Estimation project?

215. Does the Work Planning And Estimation project have a formal Work Planning And Estimation project Plan?

216. What weaknesses do you have?

217. Are requirements management tracking tools and procedures in place?

218. What threats might prevent you from getting there?

219. Does the document/deliverable meet all requirements (for example, statement of work) specific to this deliverable?

220. What do you audit?

2.8 Work Breakdown Structure: Work Planning And Estimation

221. How big is a work-package?

222. Can you make it?

223. When do you stop?

224. How far down?

225. How will you and your Work Planning And Estimation project team define the Work Planning And Estimation projects scope and work breakdown structure?

226. Where does it take place?

227. When would you develop a Work Breakdown Structure?

228. What is the probability that the Work Planning And Estimation project duration will exceed xx weeks?

229. When does it have to be done?

230. Is the work breakdown structure (wbs) defined and is the scope of the Work Planning And Estimation project clear with assigned deliverable owners?

231. How much detail?

232. Why is it useful?

233. Who has to do it?

234. What has to be done?

235. What is the probability of completing the Work Planning And Estimation project in less that xx days?

236. How many levels?

2.9 WBS Dictionary: Work Planning And Estimation

237. Are data elements (BCWS, BCWP, and ACWP) progressively summarized from the detail level to the contract level through the CWBS?

238. Are work packages assigned to performing organizations?

239. Does the accounting system provide a basis for auditing records of direct costs chargeable to the contract?

240. Does the contractor have procedures which permit identification of recurring or non-recurring costs as necessary?

241. Are the latest revised estimates of costs at completion compared with the established budgets at appropriate levels and causes of variances identified?

242. Does the contractors system include procedures for measuring the performance of critical subcontractors?

243. Are the overhead pools formally and adequately identified?

244. Are work packages reasonably short in time duration or do they have adequate objective indicators/milestones to minimize subjectivity of the

in process work evaluation?

245. Are all affected work authorizations, budgeting, and scheduling documents amended to properly reflect the effects of authorized changes?

246. Are budgets or values assigned to work packages and planning packages in terms of dollars, hours, or other measurable units?

247. Are current budgets resulting from changes to the authorized work and/or internal replanning, reconcilable to original budgets for specified reporting items?

248. Are the variances between budgeted and actual indirect costs identified and analyzed at the level of assigned responsibility for control (indirect pool, department, etc.)?

249. Changes in the current direct and Work Planning And Estimation projected base?

250. Can the contractor substantiate work package and planning package budgets?

251. Where learning is used in developing underlying budgets is there a direct relationship between anticipated learning and time phased budgets?

252. Are records maintained to show full accountability for all material purchased for the contract, including the residual inventory?

253. Is budgeted cost for work performed calculated in a manner consistent with the way work is planned?

254. Is each control account assigned to a single organizational element directly responsible for the work and identifiable to a single element of the CWBS?

255. Is the work done on a work package level as described in the WBS dictionary?

2.10 Schedule Management Plan: Work Planning And Estimation

256. Has your organization readiness assessment been conducted?

257. Goal: is the schedule feasible and at what cost?

258. Is the schedule updated on a periodic basis?

259. Are tasks tracked by hours?

260. Are corrective actions and variances reported?

261. Is documentation created for communication with the suppliers and Vendors?

262. Alignment to strategic goals & objectives?

263. Are all payments made according to the contract(s)?

264. Are all key components of a Quality Assurance Plan present?

265. Are actuals compared against estimates to analyze and correct variances?

266. Has the ims content been baselined and is it adequately controlled?

267. Will the tools selected accomplish the scheduling needs?

268. Are procurement deliverables arriving on time and to specification?

269. Are the people assigned to the Work Planning And Estimation project sufficiently qualified?

270. Have reserves been created to address risks?

271. Are the quality tools and methods identified in the Quality Plan appropriate to the Work Planning And Estimation project?

272. Are Work Planning And Estimation project leaders committed to this Work Planning And Estimation project full time?

273. Is there an onboarding process in place?

274. Does the schedule have reasonable float?

2.11 Activity List: Work Planning And Estimation

275. What will be performed?

276. What is the LF and LS for each activity?

277. Where will it be performed?

278. What went right?

279. When do the individual activities need to start and finish?

280. How can the Work Planning And Estimation project be displayed graphically to better visualize the activities?

281. Who will perform the work?

282. What are the critical bottleneck activities?

283. How detailed should a Work Planning And Estimation project get?

284. In what sequence?

285. What is the probability the Work Planning And Estimation project can be completed in xx weeks?

286. Can you determine the activity that must finish, before this activity can start?

287. How much slack is available in the Work Planning And Estimation project?

288. Are the required resources available or need to be acquired?

289. How will it be performed?

290. When will the work be performed?

291. What are you counting on?

292. What is the total time required to complete the Work Planning And Estimation project if no delays occur?

293. What is your organizations history in doing similar activities?

2.12 Activity Attributes: Work Planning And Estimation

294. Resources to accomplish the work?

295. What is the general pattern here?

296. Do you feel very comfortable with your prediction?

297. What is missing?

298. How else could the items be grouped?

299. How many resources do you need to complete the work scope within a limit of X number of days?

300. What conclusions/generalizations can you draw from this?

301. Were there other ways you could have organized the data to achieve similar results?

302. Activity: what is Missing?

303. Are the required resources available?

304. Where else does it apply?

305. Is there anything planned that does not need to be here?

306. Why?

307. How much activity detail is required?

308. How difficult will it be to do specific activities on this Work Planning And Estimation project?

309. Is there a trend during the year?

310. Have constraints been applied to the start and finish milestones for the phases?

2.13 Milestone List: Work Planning And Estimation

311. Effects on core activities, distraction?

312. Describe the industry you are in and the market growth opportunities. What is the market for your technology, product or service?

313. Identify critical paths (one or more) and which activities are on the critical path?

314. Calculate how long can activity be delayed?

315. What is the market for your technology, product or service?

316. What has been done so far?

317. Loss of key staff?

318. Sustaining internal capabilities?

319. Who will manage the Work Planning And Estimation project on a day-to-day basis?

320. How soon can the activity finish?

321. How late can each activity be finished and started?

322. Gaps in capabilities?

323. Describe the concept of the technology, product or service that will be or has been developed. How will it be used?

324. What date will the task finish?

325. Do you foresee any technical risks or developmental challenges?

326. Can you derive how soon can the whole Work Planning And Estimation project finish?

327. Legislative effects?

328. Global influences?

329. Information and research?

2.14 Network Diagram: Work Planning And Estimation

330. What job or jobs precede it?

331. What are the tools?

332. What controls the start and finish of a job?

333. Where do schedules come from?

334. How confident can you be in your milestone dates and the delivery date?

335. What must be completed before an activity can be started?

336. What activity must be completed immediately before this activity can start?

337. Are the gantt chart and/or network diagram updated periodically and used to assess the overall Work Planning And Estimation project timetable?

338. What are the Major Administrative Issues?

339. How difficult will it be to do specific activities on this Work Planning And Estimation project?

340. What job or jobs could run concurrently?

341. Why must you schedule milestones, such as reviews, throughout the Work Planning And

Estimation project?

342. What is the probability of completing the Work Planning And Estimation project in less that xx days?

343. What activities must occur simultaneously with this activity?

344. What to do and When?

345. Review the logical flow of the network diagram. Take a look at which activities you have first and then sequence the activities. Do they make sense?

346. If the Work Planning And Estimation project network diagram cannot change and you have extra personnel resources, what is the BEST thing to do?

2.15 Activity Resource Requirements: Work Planning And Estimation

347. Do you use tools like decomposition and rolling-wave planning to produce the activity list and other outputs?

348. Time for overtime?

349. Are there unresolved issues that need to be addressed?

350. How many signatures do you require on a check and does this match what is in your policy and procedures?

351. Which logical relationship does the PDM use most often?

352. Anything else?

353. How do you manage time?

354. Other support in specific areas?

355. What are constraints that you might find during the Human Resource Planning process?

356. What is the Work Plan Standard?

357. Why do you do that?

358. When does monitoring begin?

359. How do you handle petty cash?

360. Organizational Applicability?

2.16 Resource Breakdown Structure: Work Planning And Estimation

361. What defines a successful Work Planning And Estimation project?

362. What defines a successful Work Planning And Estimation project?

363. What is the purpose of assigning and documenting responsibility?

364. Who needs what information?

365. How should the information be delivered?

366. Which resource planning tool provides information on resource responsibility and accountability?

367. Who will use the system?

368. Who is allowed to perform which functions?

369. What is the primary purpose of the human resource plan?

370. Goals for the Work Planning And Estimation project. What is each stakeholders desired outcome for the Work Planning And Estimation project?

371. How difficult will it be to do specific activities on this Work Planning And Estimation project?

372. The list could probably go on, but, the thing that you would most like to know is, How long & How much?

373. Any changes from stakeholders?

374. Why do you do it?

375. What are the requirements for resource data?

376. Is predictive resource analysis being done?

377. Which resources should be in the resource pool?

2.17 Activity Duration Estimates: Work Planning And Estimation

378. How does Work Planning And Estimation project integration management relate to the Work Planning And Estimation project life cycle, stakeholders, and the other Work Planning And Estimation project management knowledge areas?

379. Consider the examples of poor quality in information technology Work Planning And Estimation projects presented in the What Went Wrong?

380. What is the shortest possible time it will take to complete this Work Planning And Estimation project?

381. What distinguishes one organization from another in this area?

382. Are Work Planning And Estimation project activities decomposed into manageable components to ensure expected management control?

383. What are the three main outputs of quality control?

384. Who will be the main sponsor for it?

385. Account for the four frames of organizations. How can they help Work Planning And Estimation project managers understand your organizational context for Work Planning And Estimation projects?

386. Are processes defined to monitor Work Planning And Estimation project cost and schedule variances?

387. Why time management?

388. What is the BEST thing for the Work Planning And Estimation project manager to do?

389. Are contingency plans created to prepare for risk events to occur?

390. Is the work performed reviewed against contractual objectives?

391. Who will promote it?

392. Do they make sense?

393. Based on , if you need to shorten the duration of the Work Planning And Estimation project, what activity would you try to shorten?

394. What are the key components of a Work Planning And Estimation project communications plan?

395. Why do you need a good WBS to use Work Planning And Estimation project management software?

396. What are the main types of contracts if you do decide to outsource?

2.18 Duration Estimating Worksheet: Work Planning And Estimation

397. When, then?

398. What utility impacts are there?

399. How should ongoing costs be monitored to try to keep the Work Planning And Estimation project within budget?

400. For other activities, how much delay can be tolerated?

401. Can the Work Planning And Estimation project be constructed as planned?

402. Value pocket identification & quantification what are value pockets?

403. Why estimate time and cost?

404. Define the work as completely as possible. What work will be included in the Work Planning And Estimation project?

405. Will the Work Planning And Estimation project collaborate with the local community and leverage resources?

406. What questions do you have?

407. Is the Work Planning And Estimation project

responsive to community need?

408. What is an Average Work Planning And Estimation project?

409. Is a construction detail attached (to aid in explanation)?

410. What info is needed?

411. Do any colleagues have experience with your organization and/or RFPs?

412. What is next?

413. Does the Work Planning And Estimation project provide innovative ways for stakeholders to overcome obstacles or deliver better outcomes?

2.19 Project Schedule: Work Planning And Estimation

414. Are procedures defined by which the Work Planning And Estimation project schedule may be changed?

415. Does the condition or event threaten the Work Planning And Estimation projects objectives in any ways?

416. If there are any qualifying green components to this Work Planning And Estimation project, what portion of the total Work Planning And Estimation project cost is green?

417. Why do you need to manage Work Planning And Estimation project Risk?

418. Month Work Planning And Estimation project take?

419. What is the difference?

420. What is risk management?

421. How much slack is available in the Work Planning And Estimation project?

422. Are you working on the right risks?

423. What is the most mis-scheduled part of process?

424. How can slack be negative?

425. Verify that the update is accurate. Are all remaining durations correct?

426. Eliminate unnecessary activities. Are there activities that came from a template or previous Work Planning And Estimation project that are not applicable on this phase of this Work Planning And Estimation project?

427. How do you know that youhave done this right?

428. Are the original Work Planning And Estimation project schedule and budget realistic?

429. To what degree is do you feel the entire team was committed to the Work Planning And Estimation project schedule?

2.20 Cost Management Plan: Work Planning And Estimation

430. Vac -variance at completion, how much over/ under budget do you expect to be?

431. Was your organizations estimating methodology being used and followed?

432. Are there checklists created to determine if all quality processes are followed?

433. Was the Work Planning And Estimation project schedule reviewed by all stakeholders and formally accepted?

434. Are risk triggers captured?

435. Are the people assigned to the Work Planning And Estimation project sufficiently qualified?

436. Is there a formal set of procedures supporting Stakeholder Management?

437. Is stakeholder involvement adequate?

438. Are trade-offs between accepting the risk and mitigating the risk identified?

439. Is the Work Planning And Estimation project schedule available for all Work Planning And Estimation project team members to review?

440. Are adequate resources provided for the quality assurance function?

441. Are the key elements of a Work Planning And Estimation project Charter present?

442. Who will prepare the cost estimates?

443. Have activity relationships and interdependencies within tasks been adequately identified?

444. Are software metrics formally captured, analyzed and used as a basis for other Work Planning And Estimation project estimates?

445. Have all necessary approvals been obtained?

446. Are changes in deliverable commitments agreed to by all affected groups & individuals?

447. Has a Work Planning And Estimation project Communications Plan been developed?

2.21 Activity Cost Estimates: Work Planning And Estimation

448. How do you do activity recasts?

449. What makes a good expected result statement?

450. Will you use any tools, such as Work Planning And Estimation project management software, to assist in capturing Earned Value metrics?

451. How do you change activities?

452. Will you need to provide essential services information about activities?

453. Is costing method consistent with study goals?

454. Measurable - are the targets measurable?

455. Eac -estimate at completion, what is the total job expected to cost?

456. Are cost subtotals needed?

457. Based on your Work Planning And Estimation project communication management plan, what worked well?

458. What is the Work Planning And Estimation projects sustainability strategy that will ensure Work Planning And Estimation project results will endure or be sustained?

459. Were the costs or charges reasonable?

460. Specific - is the objective clear in terms of what, how, when, and where the situation will be changed?

461. What areas were overlooked on this Work Planning And Estimation project?

462. How do you treat administrative costs in the activity inventory?

463. Maintenance Reserve?

464. Does the activity serve a common type of customer?

465. What are the audit requirements?

466. Is there anything unique in this Work Planning And Estimation projects scope statement that will affect resources?

2.22 Cost Estimating Worksheet: Work Planning And Estimation

467. What additional Work Planning And Estimation project(s) could be initiated as a result of this Work Planning And Estimation project?

468. Can a trend be established from historical performance data on the selected measure and are the criteria for using trend analysis or forecasting methods met?

469. How will the results be shared and to whom?

470. Who is best positioned to know and assist in identifying corresponding factors?

471. What will others want?

472. What can be included?

473. Does the Work Planning And Estimation project provide innovative ways for stakeholders to overcome obstacles or deliver better outcomes?

474. What is the estimated labor cost today based upon this information?

475. What costs are to be estimated?

476. Is it feasible to establish a control group arrangement?

477. What is the purpose of estimating?

478. Ask: are others positioned to know, are others credible, and will others cooperate?

479. What happens to any remaining funds not used?

480. Will the Work Planning And Estimation project collaborate with the local community and leverage resources?

481. Identify the timeframe necessary to monitor progress and collect data to determine how the selected measure has changed?

482. Is the Work Planning And Estimation project responsive to community need?

2.23 Cost Baseline: Work Planning And Estimation

483. Is the requested change request a result of changes in other Work Planning And Estimation project(s)?

484. Have the lessons learned been filed with the Work Planning And Estimation project Management Office?

485. Are procedures defined by which the cost baseline may be changed?

486. How difficult will it be to do specific tasks on the Work Planning And Estimation project?

487. What is the consequence?

488. What do you want to measure ?

489. What deliverables come first?

490. What is the reality?

491. Have the actual milestone completion dates been compared to the approved schedule?

492. How do you manage cost?

493. Impact to environment?

494. Does the suggested change request seem to

represent a necessary enhancement to the product?

495. Have all approved changes to the cost baseline been identified and impact on the Work Planning And Estimation project documented?

496. Have all approved changes to the schedule baseline been identified and impact on the Work Planning And Estimation project documented?

497. Has the Work Planning And Estimation project (or Work Planning And Estimation project phase) been evaluated against each objective established in the product description and Integrated Work Planning And Estimation project Plan?

498. How will cost estimates be used?

499. Are you asking management for something as a result of this update?

2.24 Quality Management Plan: Work Planning And Estimation

500. Does a prospective decision remain the same regardless of what the data show is?

501. Are you meeting the quality standards?

502. How are deviations from procedures handled?

503. What type of in-house testing do you conduct?

504. How is equipment calibrated?

505. What are your results for key measures/indicators of accomplishment of organizational strategy?

506. What are your organizations current levels and trends for the already stated measures related to financial and marketplace performance?

507. Does the program conduct field testing?

508. Documented results available?

509. Account for the procedures used to verify the data quality of the data being reviewed?

510. Does the Work Planning And Estimation project have a formal Work Planning And Estimation project Plan?

511. Have all involved stakeholders and work groups

committed to the Work Planning And Estimation project?

512. How are calibration records kept?

513. No superfluous information or marketing narrative?

514. How do senior leaders create and communicate values and performance expectations?

515. Who is responsible?

516. Is the steering committee active in Work Planning And Estimation project oversight?

517. Is this process still needed?

518. How are your organizations compensation and recognition approaches and the performance management system used to reinforce high performance?

519. How does your organization design processes to ensure others meet customer and others requirements?

2.25 Quality Metrics: Work Planning And Estimation

520. What is the timeline to meet your goal?

521. Is the reporting frequency appropriate?

522. Subjective quality component: customer satisfaction, how do you measure it?

523. How do you know if everyone is trying to improve the right things?

524. What percentage are outcome-based?

525. What happens if you get an abnormal result?

526. How are requirements conflicts resolved?

527. Did the team meet the Work Planning And Estimation project success criteria documented in the Quality Metrics Matrix?

528. How do you calculate corresponding metrics?

529. Are applicable standards referenced and available?

530. What metrics do you measure?

531. Has trace of defects been initiated?

532. What makes a visualization memorable?

533. What do you measure?

534. Is there alignment within your organization on definitions?

535. What forces exist that would cause them to change?

536. How do you calculate such metrics?

537. Are quality metrics defined?

2.26 Process Improvement Plan: Work Planning And Estimation

538. What personnel are the sponsors for that initiative?

539. Are you making progress on the goals?

540. Has a process guide to collect the data been developed?

541. Have storage and access mechanisms and procedures been determined?

542. To elicit goal statements, do you ask a question such as, What do you want to achieve?

543. What personnel are the champions for the initiative?

544. What personnel are the coaches for your initiative?

545. Does explicit definition of the measures exist?

546. What lessons have you learned so far?

547. Does your process ensure quality?

548. Have the supporting tools been developed or acquired?

549. Purpose of goal: the motive is determined by

asking, why do you want to achieve this goal?

550. Are you making progress on the improvement framework?

551. Where are you now?

552. Modeling current processes is great, and will you ever see a return on that investment?

553. Where do you want to be?

554. Why do you want to achieve the goal?

555. What is the return on investment?

556. Management commitment at all levels?

2.27 Responsibility Assignment Matrix: Work Planning And Estimation

557. Do you need to convince people that its well worth the time and effort?

558. Do all the identified groups or people really need to be consulted?

559. The staff interests – is the group or the person interested in working for this Work Planning And Estimation project?

560. What tool can show you individual and group allocations?

561. Budgets assigned to control accounts?

562. What do you need to implement earned value management?

563. Are people encouraged to bring up issues?

564. Do others have the time to dedicate to your Work Planning And Estimation project?

565. Are detailed work packages planned as far in advance as practicable?

566. Are authorized changes being incorporated in a timely manner?

567. Is work progressively subdivided into detailed

work packages as requirements are defined?

568. Changes in the overhead pool and/or organization structures?

569. Are records maintained to show how undistributed budgets are controlled?

570. Budgeted cost for work performed?

571. Is work properly classified as measured effort, LOE, or apportioned effort and appropriately separated?

572. Are the actual costs used for variance analysis reconcilable with data from the accounting system?

573. When performing is split among two or more roles, is the work clearly defined so that the efforts are coordinated and the communication is clear?

574. Does the contractor use objective results, design reviews and tests to trace schedule performance?

2.28 Roles and Responsibilities: Work Planning And Estimation

575. Who is responsible for each task?

576. Influence: what areas of organizational decision making are you able to influence when you do not have authority to make the final decision?

577. What specific behaviors did you observe?

578. What areas would you highlight for changes or improvements?

579. What should you highlight for improvement?

580. Have you ever been a part of this team?

581. Once the responsibilities are defined for the Work Planning And Estimation project, have the deliverables, roles and responsibilities been clearly communicated to every participant?

582. Is there a training program in place for stakeholders covering expectations, roles and responsibilities and any addition knowledge others need to be good stakeholders?

583. How is your work-life balance?

584. How well did the Work Planning And Estimation project Team understand the expectations of specific roles and responsibilities?

585. Once the responsibilities are defined for the Work Planning And Estimation project, have the deliverables, roles and responsibilities been clearly communicated to every participant?

586. Are governance roles and responsibilities documented?

587. What areas of supervision are challenging for you?

588. What expectations were NOT met?

589. Key conclusions and recommendations: Are conclusions and recommendations relevant and acceptable?

590. What are your major roles and responsibilities in the area of performance measurement and assessment?

591. Do you take the time to clearly define roles and responsibilities on Work Planning And Estimation project tasks?

592. What should you do now to prepare for your career 5+ years from now?

593. What should you do now to prepare yourself for a promotion, increased responsibilities or a different job?

2.29 Human Resource Management Plan: Work Planning And Estimation

594. What talent is needed?

595. Are decisions captured in a decisions log?

596. What skills, knowledge and experiences are required?

597. What were things that you need to improve?

598. Responsiveness to change and the resulting demands for different skills and abilities?

599. Was the scope definition used in task sequencing?

600. Has a quality assurance plan been developed for the Work Planning And Estimation project?

601. Is there an approved case?

602. Is an industry recognized support tool(s) being used for Work Planning And Estimation project scheduling & tracking?

603. Are metrics used to evaluate and manage Vendors?

604. Was the Work Planning And Estimation project schedule reviewed by all stakeholders and formally accepted?

605. Are the Work Planning And Estimation project plans updated on a frequent basis?

606. How will the Work Planning And Estimation project manage expectations & meet needs and requirements?

607. What commitments have been made?

608. Have Work Planning And Estimation project success criteria been defined?

609. Is the Work Planning And Estimation project schedule available for all Work Planning And Estimation project team members to review?

610. Have Work Planning And Estimation project management standards and procedures been identified / established and documented?

611. Does the Work Planning And Estimation project have a Statement of Work?

2.30 Communications Management Plan: Work Planning And Estimation

612. Who have you worked with in past, similar initiatives?

613. Who will use or be affected by the result of a Work Planning And Estimation project?

614. Do you prepare stakeholder engagement plans?

615. Are there too many who have an interest in some aspect of your work?

616. Can you think of other people who might have concerns or interests?

617. What to learn?

618. Are you constantly rushing from meeting to meeting?

619. What is the stakeholders level of authority?

620. Which stakeholders are thought leaders, influences, or early adopters?

621. Who to learn from?

622. Who is involved as you identify stakeholders?

623. Are the stakeholders getting the information others need, are others consulted, are concerns

addressed?

624. Who were proponents/opponents?

625. Who did you turn to if you had questions?

626. Where do team members get information?

627. Which team member will work with each stakeholder?

628. Do you feel more overwhelmed by stakeholders?

629. How is this initiative related to other portfolios, programs, or Work Planning And Estimation projects?

630. What are the interrelationships?

631. What to know?

2.31 Risk Management Plan: Work Planning And Estimation

632. What will drive change?

633. What is the probability the risk avoidance strategy will be successful?

634. Does the Work Planning And Estimation project team have experience with the technology to be implemented?

635. Are the metrics meaningful and useful?

636. Which risks should get the attention?

637. Are tool mentors available?

638. Methodology: how will risk management be performed on this Work Planning And Estimation project?

639. Are the required plans included, such as nonstructural flood risk management plans?

640. Are requirements fully understood by the software engineering team and customers?

641. Could others have been better mitigated?

642. Why might it be late?

643. Are the software tools integrated with each

other?

644. Are the best people available?

645. What things might go wrong?

646. Do you have a consistent repeatable process that is actually used?

647. Should the risk be taken at all?

648. What are the cost, schedule and resource impacts if the risk does occur?

649. How do you manage Work Planning And Estimation project Risk?

650. Is a software Work Planning And Estimation project management tool available?

651. Internal technical and management reviews?

2.32 Risk Register: Work Planning And Estimation

652. Recovery actions - planned actions taken once a risk has occurred to allow you to move on. What should you do after?

653. When would you develop a risk register?

654. Assume the event happens, what is the Most Likely impact?

655. What should you do now?

656. How well are risks controlled?

657. Risk categories: what are the main categories of risks that should be addressed on this Work Planning And Estimation project?

658. Assume the risk event or situation happens, what would the impact be?

659. Risk probability and impact: how will the probabilities and impacts of risk items be assessed?

660. What evidence do you have to justify the likelihood score of the risk (audit, incident report, claim, complaints, inspection, internal review)?

661. Amongst the action plans and recommendations that you have to introduce are there some that could stop or delay the overall program?

662. Are there other alternative controls that could be implemented?

663. Why would you develop a risk register?

664. Methodology: how will risk management be performed on this Work Planning And Estimation project?

665. Are your objectives at risk?

666. Financial risk -can your organization afford to undertake the Work Planning And Estimation project?

667. User involvement: do you have the right users?

668. Does the evidence highlight any areas to advance opportunities or foster good relations. If yes what steps will be taken?

669. What is a Risk?

670. Who is accountable?

2.33 Probability and Impact Assessment: Work Planning And Estimation

671. Risks should be identified during which phase of Work Planning And Estimation project management life cycle?

672. Are the risk data timely and relevant?

673. Does the customer have a solid idea of what is required?

674. Are tools for analysis and design available?

675. Will there be an increase in the political conservatism?

676. Do you use any methods to analyze risks?

677. What will be the environmental impact of the Work Planning And Estimation project?

678. Your customers business requirements have suddenly shifted because of a new regulatory statute, what now?

679. What significant shift will occur in governmental policies, laws, and regulations pertaining to specific industries?

680. What risks are necessary to achieve success?

681. How much is the probability of a risk occurring?

682. Can this technology be absorbed with current level of expertise available in your organization?

683. What should be the level of coordination?

684. What should be done with non-critical risks?

685. Risk urgency assessment -which of your risks could occur soon, or require a longer planning time?

686. Do benefits and chances of success outweigh potential damage if success is not attained?

687. Are the risk data complete?

688. How well is the risk understood?

689. Do you have specific methods that you use for each phase of the process?

2.34 Probability and Impact Matrix: Work Planning And Estimation

690. Amount of reused software?

691. How much risk do others need to take?

692. Is the delay in one subWork Planning And Estimation project going to affect another?

693. How is the Work Planning And Estimation project going to be managed?

694. How do risks change during the Work Planning And Estimation projects life cycle?

695. What are the ways you measure and evaluate risks?

696. What is the best method for analysing the risks for different types of Work Planning And Estimation projects?

697. Is the Work Planning And Estimation project cutting across the entire organization?

698. What can you use the analyzed risks for?

699. Does the Work Planning And Estimation project team have experience with the technology to be implemented?

700. Do requirements demand the use of new

analysis, design, or testing methods?

701. Premium on reliability of product?

702. Can the risk be avoided by choosing a different alternative?

703. My Work Planning And Estimation project leader has suddenly left your organization, what do you do?

704. Has the need for the Work Planning And Estimation project been properly established?

705. How should you structure risks?

706. What would be the best solution?

707. Mandated delivery date?

708. What did not work so well?

2.35 Risk Data Sheet: Work Planning And Estimation

709. What is the likelihood of it happening?

710. What actions can be taken to eliminate or remove risk?

711. What will be the consequences if the risk happens?

712. What are the main opportunities available to you that you should grab while you can?

713. How can hazards be reduced?

714. Whom do you serve (customers)?

715. Type of risk identified?

716. Do effective diagnostic tests exist?

717. What are the main threats to your existence?

718. How can it happen?

719. Risk of what?

720. What were the Causes that contributed?

721. What can happen?

722. Potential for recurrence?

723. How reliable is the data source?

724. Has a sensitivity analysis been carried out?

725. What do people affected think about the need for, and practicality of preventive measures?

726. What are you trying to achieve (Objectives)?

727. What do you know?

2.36 Procurement Management Plan: Work Planning And Estimation

728. Have adequate resources been provided by management to ensure Work Planning And Estimation project success?

729. Is the steering committee active in Work Planning And Estimation project oversight?

730. Are vendor contract reports, reviews and visits conducted periodically?

731. Is it standard practice to formally commit stakeholders to the Work Planning And Estimation project via agreements?

732. Is there a Steering Committee in place?

733. Do Work Planning And Estimation project managers participating in the Work Planning And Estimation project know the Work Planning And Estimation projects true status first hand?

734. If standardized procurement documents are needed, where can others be found?

735. Is there a procurement management plan in place?

736. If independent estimates will be needed as evaluation criteria, who will prepare them and when?

737. Are the people assigned to the Work Planning And Estimation project sufficiently qualified?

2.37 Source Selection Criteria: Work Planning And Estimation

738. How should the oral presentations be handled?

739. Is a letter of commitment from each proposed team member and key subcontractor included?

740. What can not be disclosed?

741. Do you ensure you evaluate what you asked for, not what you want to see or expect to see?

742. How can the methods of publicizing the buy be tailored to yield more effective price competition?

743. How should oral presentations be evaluated?

744. What evidence should be provided regarding proposal evaluations?

745. Is the contracting office likely to receive more purchase requests for this item or service during the coming year?

746. Can you prevent comparison of proposals?

747. Who is entitled to a debriefing?

748. Is this a cost contract?

749. How should the preproposal conference be conducted?

750. Does the evaluation of any change include an impact analysis; how will the change affect the scope, time, cost, and quality of the goods or services being provided?

751. What are open book debriefings?

752. What should preproposal conferences accomplish?

753. How should oral presentations be prepared for?

754. How important is cost in the source selection decision relative to past performance and technical considerations?

755. Are there any common areas of weaknesses or deficiencies in the proposals in the competitive range?

756. With the rapid changes in information technology, will media be readable in five or ten years?

757. What risks were identified in the proposals?

2.38 Stakeholder Management Plan: Work Planning And Estimation

758. Is there an on-going process in place to monitor Work Planning And Estimation project risks?

759. Is there general agreement & acceptance of the current status and progress of the Work Planning And Estimation project?

760. Is there a requirements change management processes in place?

761. Is the performance of the supplier to be rated and documented?

762. Has the Work Planning And Estimation project manager been identified?

763. Is the communication plan being followed?

764. Are meeting minutes captured and sent out after the meeting?

765. Have process improvement efforts been completed before requirements efforts begin?

766. Have all team members been part of identifying risks?

767. Are there nonconformance issues?

768. Are all resource assumptions documented?

769. How are stakeholders chosen and what roles might they have on a Work Planning And Estimation project?

770. Does the Work Planning And Estimation project have a formal Work Planning And Estimation project Charter?

771. Are parking lot items captured?

772. Are software metrics formally captured, analyzed and used as a basis for other Work Planning And Estimation project estimates?

773. Do you know what your customers expectations are regarding this process?

2.39 Change Management Plan: Work Planning And Estimation

774. Where will the funds come from?

775. Has a training need analysis been carried out?

776. What are the needs, priorities and special interests of the audience?

777. Who in the business it includes?

778. Is there a need for new relationships to be built?

779. What will be the preferred method of delivery?

780. Who will fund the training?

781. What work practices will be affected?

782. Who might present the most resistance?

783. Will the readiness criteria be met prior to the training roll out?

784. Have the business unit contacts been selected and notified?

785. What is going to be done differently?

786. What is the worst thing that can happen if you communicate information?

787. Is there a support model for this application and are the details available for distribution?

788. How do you know the requirements you documented are the right ones?

789. How does the principle of senders and receivers make the Work Planning And Estimation project communications effort more complex?

790. Are work location changes required?

791. What prerequisite knowledge or training is required?

792. What relationships will change?

3.0 Executing Process Group: Work Planning And Estimation

793. How can your organization use a weighted decision matrix to evaluate proposals as part of source selection?

794. What are the Work Planning And Estimation project management deliverables of each process group?

795. When is the appropriate time to bring the scorecard to Board meetings?

796. Do your results resemble a normal distribution?

797. How many different communication channels does the Work Planning And Estimation project team have?

798. Do schedule issues conflicts?

799. What are the key components of the Work Planning And Estimation project communications plan?

800. What is the product of your Work Planning And Estimation project?

801. How will professionals learn what is expected from them what the deliverables are?

802. What areas does the group agree are the biggest

success on the Work Planning And Estimation project?

803. What does it mean to take a systems view of a Work Planning And Estimation project?

804. What is the difference between using brainstorming and the Delphi technique for risk identification?

805. Do the partners have sufficient financial capacity to keep up the benefits produced by the programme?

806. Are decisions made in a timely manner?

807. Do the products created live up to the necessary quality?

808. How do you enter durations, link tasks, and view critical path information?

809. Is the schedule for the set products being met?

810. In what way has the program come up with innovative measures for problem-solving?

811. Is the Work Planning And Estimation project making progress in helping to achieve the set results?

3.1 Team Member Status Report: Work Planning And Estimation

812. Does every department have to have a Work Planning And Estimation project Manager on staff?

813. Will the staff do training or is that done by a third party?

814. Do you have an Enterprise Work Planning And Estimation project Management Office (EPMO)?

815. Is there evidence that staff is taking a more professional approach toward management of your organizations Work Planning And Estimation projects?

816. How does this product, good, or service meet the needs of the Work Planning And Estimation project and your organization as a whole?

817. Does the product, good, or service already exist within your organization?

818. When a teams productivity and success depend on collaboration and the efficient flow of information, what generally fails them?

819. What specific interest groups do you have in place?

820. What is to be done?

821. How much risk is involved?

822. Does your organization have the means (staff, money, contract, etc.) to produce or to acquire the product, good, or service?

823. Why is it to be done?

824. Are your organizations Work Planning And Estimation projects more successful over time?

825. How will resource planning be done?

826. Are the products of your organizations Work Planning And Estimation projects meeting customers objectives?

827. The problem with Reward & Recognition Programs is that the truly deserving people all too often get left out. How can you make it practical?

828. How it is to be done?

829. How can you make it practical?

830. Are the attitudes of staff regarding Work Planning And Estimation project work improving?

3.2 Change Request: Work Planning And Estimation

831. When to submit a change request?

832. What are the duties of the change control team?

833. What are the requirements for urgent changes?

834. How are the measures for carrying out the change established?

835. Will all change requests and current status be logged?

836. How does your organization control changes before and after software is released to a customer?

837. Will all change requests be unconditionally tracked through this process?

838. Why were your requested changes rejected or not made?

839. Will the change use memory to the extent that other functions will be not have sufficient memory to operate effectively?

840. Are there requirements attributes that are strongly related to the occurrence of defects and failures?

841. How do team members communicate with each

other?

842. Who needs to approve change requests?

843. How can changes be graded?

844. What is the purpose of change control?

845. What should be regulated in a change control operating instruction?

846. Screen shots or attachments included in a Change Request?

847. What is the function of the change control committee?

848. How shall the implementation of changes be recorded?

849. Have all related configuration items been properly updated?

850. Has the change been highlighted and documented in the CSCI?

3.3 Change Log: Work Planning And Estimation

851. Is the change backward compatible without limitations?

852. When was the request approved?

853. How does this change affect the timeline of the schedule?

854. Who initiated the change request?

855. Is the change request within Work Planning And Estimation project scope?

856. Is this a mandatory replacement?

857. Should a more thorough impact analysis be conducted?

858. When was the request submitted?

859. Is the change request open, closed or pending?

860. Is the requested change request a result of changes in other Work Planning And Estimation project(s)?

861. Will the Work Planning And Estimation project fail if the change request is not executed?

862. Is the submitted change a new change or a

modification of a previously approved change?

863. How does this relate to the standards developed for specific business processes?

864. How does this change affect scope?

865. Does the suggested change request represent a desired enhancement to the products functionality?

866. Do the described changes impact on the integrity or security of the system?

867. Where do changes come from?

3.4 Decision Log: Work Planning And Estimation

868. Adversarial environment. is your opponent open to a non-traditional workflow, or will it likely challenge anything you do?

869. What makes you different or better than others companies selling the same thing?

870. What alternatives/risks were considered?

871. It becomes critical to track and periodically revisit both operational effectiveness; Are you noticing all that you need to, and are you interpreting what you see effectively?

872. How do you define success?

873. Which variables make a critical difference?

874. How does an increasing emphasis on cost containment influence the strategies and tactics used?

875. What is the average size of your matters in an applicable measurement?

876. How effective is maintaining the log at facilitating organizational learning?

877. What is your overall strategy for quality control / quality assurance procedures?

878. Who is the decisionmaker?

879. How does provision of information, both in terms of content and presentation, influence acceptance of alternative strategies?

880. Who will be given a copy of this document and where will it be kept?

881. What are the cost implications?

882. Do strategies and tactics aimed at less than full control reduce the costs of management or simply shift the cost burden?

883. Does anything need to be adjusted?

884. Is everything working as expected?

885. With whom was the decision shared or considered?

886. What eDiscovery problem or issue did your organization set out to fix or make better?

887. Is your opponent open to a non-traditional workflow, or will it likely challenge anything you do?

3.5 Quality Audit: Work Planning And Estimation

888. How does your organization know that the review processes are effective?

889. Are goals well supported with strategies, operational plans, manuals and training?

890. What happens if your organization fails its Quality Audit?

891. How does your organization know that its system for recruiting the best staff possible are appropriately effective and constructive?

892. Have personnel cleanliness and health requirements been established?

893. Are training programs documented?

894. Does the audit organization have experience in performing the required work for entities of your type and size?

895. Has a written procedure been established to identify devices during all stages of receipt, reconditioning, distribution and installation so that mix-ups are prevented?

896. How does your organization know that its risk management system is appropriately effective and constructive?

897. How does your organization know that the research supervision provided to its staff is appropriately effective and constructive?

898. How does your organization know that its research funding systems are appropriately effective and constructive in enabling quality research outcomes?

899. Is progress against the intentions measurable?

900. Are salvageable and salvaged medical devices stored in a manner to prevent damage and/or contamination?

901. Do all staff have the necessary authority and resources to deliver what is expected of them?

902. Is there a written corporate quality policy?

903. How does your organization know that it is appropriately effective and constructive in preparing its staff for organizational aspirations?

904. Does the report read coherently?

905. How does your organization know that the support for its staff is appropriately effective and constructive?

906. How does your organization know that the range and quality of its accommodation, catering and transportation services are appropriately effective and constructive?

907. How does your organization know that its public relations and marketing systems are appropriately effective and constructive?

3.6 Team Directory: Work Planning And Estimation

908. Contract requirements complied with?

909. How will you accomplish and manage the objectives?

910. Process decisions: are there any statutory or regulatory issues relevant to the timely execution of work?

911. Who will report Work Planning And Estimation project status to all stakeholders?

912. When will you produce deliverables?

913. Is construction on schedule?

914. Why is the work necessary?

915. Who should receive information (all stakeholders)?

916. Process decisions: do job conditions warrant additional actions to collect job information and document on-site activity?

917. What are you going to deliver or accomplish?

918. Days from the time the issue is identified?

919. Who are the Team Members?

920. Process decisions: are all start-up, turn over and close out requirements of the contract satisfied?

921. Have you decided when to celebrate the Work Planning And Estimation projects completion date?

922. Process decisions: which organizational elements and which individuals will be assigned management functions?

923. Who are your stakeholders (customers, sponsors, end users, team members)?

924. Does a Work Planning And Estimation project team directory list all resources assigned to the Work Planning And Estimation project?

925. What needs to be communicated?

926. How do unidentified risks impact the outcome of the Work Planning And Estimation project?

3.7 Team Operating Agreement: Work Planning And Estimation

927. What are the current caseload numbers in the unit?

928. Did you delegate tasks such as taking meeting minutes, presenting a topic and soliciting input?

929. What individual strengths does each team member bring to the group?

930. Do you listen for voice tone and word choice to understand the meaning behind words?

931. Do you solicit member feedback about meetings and what would make them better?

932. Do you brief absent members after they view meeting notes or listen to a recording?

933. Are there more than two native languages represented by your team?

934. Why does your organization want to participate in teaming?

935. Are there differences in access to communication and collaboration technology based on team member location?

936. Are there the right people on your team?

937. Did you draft the meeting agenda?

938. Do you call or email participants to ensure understanding, follow-through and commitment to the meeting outcomes?

939. Do you upload presentation materials in advance and test the technology?

940. Are there more than two functional areas represented by your team?

941. Conflict resolution: how will disputes and other conflicts be mediated or resolved?

942. Did you recap the meeting purpose, time, and expectations?

943. Reimbursements: how will the team members be reimbursed for expenses and time commitments?

944. Seconds for members to respond?

945. The method to be used in the decision making process; Will it be consensus, majority rule, or the supervisor having the final say?

946. What are some potential sources of conflict among team members?

3.8 Team Performance Assessment: Work Planning And Estimation

947. To what degree do members understand and articulate the same purpose without relying on ambiguous abstractions?

948. Do friends perform better than acquaintances?

949. To what degree do members articulate the goals beyond the team membership?

950. Lack of method variance in self-reported affect and perceptions at work: Reality or artifact?

951. To what degree can team members frequently and easily communicate with one another?

952. If you are worried about method variance before you collect data, what sort of design elements might you include to reduce or eliminate the threat of method variance?

953. Do you promptly inform members about major developments that may affect them?

954. To what degree can team members vigorously define the teams purpose in considerations with others who are not part of the functioning team?

955. How do you keep key people outside the group informed about its accomplishments?

956. Individual task proficiency and team process behavior: what is important for team functioning?

957. Effects of crew composition on crew performance: Does the whole equal the sum of its parts?

958. To what degree do all members feel responsible for all agreed-upon measures?

959. Social categorization and intergroup behaviour: Does minimal intergroup discrimination make social identity more positive?

960. How much interpersonal friction is there in your team?

961. To what degree are the skill areas critical to team performance present?

962. What are teams?

963. To what degree does the teams purpose constitute a broader, deeper aspiration than just accomplishing short-term goals?

964. To what degree does the teams work approach provide opportunity for members to engage in open interaction?

965. To what degree will the team ensure that all members equitably share the work essential to the success of the team?

966. What structural changes have you made or are you preparing to make?

3.9 Team Member Performance Assessment: Work Planning And Estimation

967. How do you currently use the time that is available?

968. To what degree do team members frequently explore the teams purpose and its implications?

969. To what degree do team members understand one anothers roles and skills?

970. How effective is training that is delivered through technology-based platforms?

971. To what degree can all members engage in open and interactive considerations?

972. Who they are?

973. What is a general description of the processes under performance measurement and assessment?

974. How do you implement Cost Reduction?

975. Are any governance changes sufficient to impact achievement?

976. What future plans (e.g., modifications) do you have for your program?

977. How often should assessments be conducted?

978. Did training work?

979. New skills/knowledge gained this year?

980. Does the rater (supervisor) have to wait for the interim or final performance assessment review to tell an employee that the employees performance is unsatisfactory?

981. How will you identify your Team Leaders?

982. How is assessment information achieved, stored?

983. How do you create a self-sustaining capacity for a collaborative culture?

984. What, if any, steps are available for employees who feel they have been unfairly or inaccurately rated?

985. To what degree are the goals ambitious?

986. How will they be formed?

3.10 Issue Log: Work Planning And Estimation

987. What is the impact on the Business Case?

988. How much time does it take to do it?

989. What is the status of the issue?

990. Who reported the issue?

991. Why not more evaluators?

992. Are the Work Planning And Estimation project issues uniquely identified, including to which product they refer?

993. What are the stakeholders interrelationships?

994. What are the typical contents?

995. What approaches to you feel are the best ones to use?

996. What steps can you take for positive relationships?

997. Is access to the Issue Log controlled?

998. Do you have members of your team responsible for certain stakeholders?

999. Which stakeholders can influence others?

1000. What is a change?

1001. Who is the stakeholder?

1002. Persistence; will users learn a work around or will they be bothered every time?

1003. Why multiple evaluators?

4.0 Monitoring and Controlling Process Group: Work Planning And Estimation

1004. Where is the Risk in the Work Planning And Estimation project?

1005. What are the goals of the program?

1006. How will staff learn how to use the deliverables?

1007. What business situation is being addressed?

1008. Just how important is your work to the overall success of the Work Planning And Estimation project?

1009. Is there sufficient time allotted between the general system design and the detailed system design phases?

1010. How can you make your needs known?

1011. What input will you be required to provide the Work Planning And Estimation project team?

1012. What is the timeline for the Work Planning And Estimation project?

1013. Key stakeholders to work with. How many potential communications channels exist on the Work Planning And Estimation project?

1014. How many more potential communications

channels were introduced by the discovery of the new stakeholders?

1015. Did the Work Planning And Estimation project team have enough people to execute the Work Planning And Estimation project plan?

1016. What is the timeline?

1017. What resources are necessary?

1018. If action is called for, what form should it take?

1019. How is Agile Work Planning And Estimation project Management done?

1020. What will you do to minimize the impact should a risk event occur?

4.1 Project Performance Report: Work Planning And Estimation

1021. To what degree will the team adopt a concrete, clearly understood, and agreed-upon approach that will result in achievement of the teams goals?

1022. How will procurement be coordinated with other Work Planning And Estimation project aspects, such as scheduling and performance reporting?

1023. What is in it for you?

1024. To what degree do the relationships of the informal organization motivate taskrelevant behavior and facilitate task completion?

1025. To what degree does the information network communicate information relevant to the task?

1026. Next Steps?

1027. To what degree does the formal organization make use of individual resources and meet individual needs?

1028. To what degree is there centralized control of information sharing?

1029. To what degree does the teams work approach provide opportunity for members to engage in fact-based problem solving?

1030. To what degree does the informal organization make use of individual resources and meet individual needs?

1031. What degree are the relative importance and priority of the goals clear to all team members?

1032. What is the degree to which rules govern information exchange between groups?

1033. What is the degree to which rules govern information exchange between individuals within your organization?

1034. How can Work Planning And Estimation project sustainability be maintained?

1035. To what degree do team members articulate the teams work approach?

4.2 Variance Analysis: Work Planning And Estimation

1036. Did an existing competitor change strategy?

1037. Wbs elements contractually specified for reporting of status to your organization (lowest level only)?

1038. Did a new competitor enter the market?

1039. Does the contractors system provide unit or lot costs when applicable?

1040. Historical experience?

1041. Is the anticipated (firm and potential) business base Work Planning And Estimation projected in a rational, consistent manner?

1042. Are management actions taken to reduce indirect costs when there are significant adverse variances?

1043. Do work packages consist of discrete tasks which are adequately described?

1044. Are data elements reconcilable between internal summary reports and reports forwarded to the stakeholders?

1045. How are material, labor, and overhead standards set?

1046. Are the wbs and organizational levels for application of the Work Planning And Estimation projected overhead costs identified?

1047. Are all budgets assigned to control accounts?

1048. How are material, labor, and overhead variances calculated and recorded?

1049. Are indirect costs charged to the appropriate indirect pools and incurring organization?

1050. Do you identify potential or actual budget-based and time-based schedule variances?

1051. Other relevant issues of Variance Analysis -selling price or gross margin?

1052. Are all cwbs elements specified for external reporting?

4.3 Earned Value Status: Work Planning And Estimation

1053. When is it going to finish?

1054. Verification is a process of ensuring that the developed system satisfies the stakeholders agreements and specifications; Are you building the product right? What do you verify?

1055. Are you hitting your Work Planning And Estimation projects targets?

1056. Where are your problem areas?

1057. Where is evidence-based earned value in your organization reported?

1058. How much is it going to cost by the finish?

1059. How does this compare with other Work Planning And Estimation projects?

1060. What is the unit of forecast value?

1061. Earned value can be used in almost any Work Planning And Estimation project situation and in almost any Work Planning And Estimation project environment. it may be used on large Work Planning And Estimation projects, medium sized Work Planning And Estimation projects, tiny Work Planning And Estimation projects (in cut-down form), complex and simple Work Planning And Estimation projects and in any market sector. some people, of course, know all about earned value, they have used it for years - but perhaps not as effectively as they could have?

1062. Validation is a process of ensuring that the developed system will actually achieve the stakeholders desired outcomes; Are you building the right product? What do you validate?

1063. If earned value management (EVM) is so good in determining the true status of a Work Planning And Estimation project and Work Planning And Estimation project its completion, why is it that hardly any one uses it in information systems related Work Planning And Estimation projects?

4.4 Risk Audit: Work Planning And Estimation

1064. What resources are needed to achieve program results?

1065. Does the adoption of a business risk audit approach change internal control documentation and testing practices?

1066. Can analytical tests provide evidence that is as strong as evidence from traditional substantive tests?

1067. Are duties out-of-class?

1068. Is there a screening process that will ensure all participants have the fitness and skills required to safely participate?

1069. Is the process supported by tools?

1070. Do the people have the right combinations of skills?

1071. Is the customer willing to establish rapid communication links with the developer?

1072. What is the Board doing to assure measurement and improve outcomes and quality and reduce avoidable adverse events?

1073. What events or circumstances could affect the achievement of your objectives?

1074. From an empirical perspective, does the business risk approach lead to a more effective audit, or simply to increased consulting revenue detrimental to audit rigor?

1075. Is your organization able to present documentary evidence in support of compliance?

1076. Who is responsible for what?

1077. Do you ensure the recommended rules of play and protocols are followed for your activity?

1078. For paid staff, does your organization comply with the minimum conditions for employment and/or the applicable modern award?

1079. Has risk management been considered when planning an event?

1080. Are all managers or operators of the facility or equipment competent or qualified?

1081. What are the benefits of a Enterprise wide approach to Risk Management?

1082. What are the risks that could stop you from achieving your objectives?

1083. Does your organization have a social media policy and procedure?

4.5 Contractor Status Report: Work Planning And Estimation

1084. What was the final actual cost?

1085. How long have you been using the services?

1086. How is risk transferred?

1087. Describe how often regular updates are made to the proposed solution. Are corresponding regular updates included in the standard maintenance plan?

1088. How does the proposed individual meet each requirement?

1089. What are the minimum and optimal bandwidth requirements for the proposed solution?

1090. What is the average response time for answering a support call?

1091. What was the overall budget or estimated cost?

1092. What was the actual budget or estimated cost for your organizations services?

1093. What was the budget or estimated cost for your organizations services?

1094. Who can list a Work Planning And Estimation project as organization experience, your organization or a previous employee of your organization?

1095. What process manages the contracts?

1096. If applicable; describe your standard schedule for new software version releases. Are new software version releases included in the standard maintenance plan?

1097. Are there contractual transfer concerns?

4.6 Formal Acceptance: Work Planning And Estimation

1098. Does it do what Work Planning And Estimation project team said it would?

1099. Do you buy-in installation services?

1100. What was done right?

1101. Does it do what client said it would?

1102. Who would use it?

1103. What are the requirements against which to test, Who will execute?

1104. How well did the team follow the methodology?

1105. What function(s) does it fill or meet?

1106. Have all comments been addressed?

1107. Was the Work Planning And Estimation project managed well?

1108. Do you perform formal acceptance or burn-in tests?

1109. How does your team plan to obtain formal acceptance on your Work Planning And Estimation project?

1110. What lessons were learned about your Work Planning And Estimation project management methodology?

1111. Who supplies data?

1112. Was the Work Planning And Estimation project goal achieved?

1113. What features, practices, and processes proved to be strengths or weaknesses?

1114. What is the Acceptance Management Process?

1115. Was business value realized?

1116. Did the Work Planning And Estimation project achieve its MOV?

1117. Is formal acceptance of the Work Planning And Estimation project product documented and distributed?

5.0 Closing Process Group: Work Planning And Estimation

1118. Mitigate. what will you do to minimize the impact should a risk event occur?

1119. How critical is the Work Planning And Estimation project success to the success of your organization?

1120. Is this a follow-on to a previous Work Planning And Estimation project?

1121. What went well?

1122. Will the Work Planning And Estimation project deliverable(s) replace a current asset or group of assets?

1123. Were cost budgets met?

1124. What was learned?

1125. Were risks identified and mitigated?

1126. How well did the team follow the chosen processes?

1127. Are there funding or time constraints?

1128. Is this an updated Work Planning And Estimation project Proposal Document?

1129. Can the lesson learned be replicated?

1130. What is the amount of funding and what Work Planning And Estimation project phases are funded?

1131. How will you know you did it?

1132. What is the Work Planning And Estimation project Management Process?

1133. What areas were overlooked on this Work Planning And Estimation project?

1134. Contingency planning. if a risk event occurs, what will you do?

5.1 Procurement Audit: Work Planning And Estimation

1135. Are known obligations, such as salaries and contracts, encumbered at the beginning of the year?

1136. Is the issuance of purchase orders scheduled so that orders are not issued daily?

1137. Is the procurement process organized the most appropriate way taking into consideration the amount of procurement?

1138. Is trend analysis performed on expenditures made by key employees and by vendor?

1139. Are approvals needed if changes are made in the quantity or specification of the original purchase requisition?

1140. How do you monitor behaviour of procurement staff?

1141. Were standards, certifications and evidence required admissible?

1142. Are prices always included on the purchase order?

1143. Is there a practice that prohibits signing blank purchase orders?

1144. Is there an effective risk management system

continuously monitoring procurement risk?

1145. Are checks used in numeric sequence?

1146. Are advantages and disadvantages of in-house production, outsourcing and Public Private Partnerships considered?

1147. Was the decision on the award process accurate and adequately communicated?

1148. Are there regular reviews and analysis of the performance of the procurement function/unit?

1149. Is the minutes book kept current?

1150. Is there a need for the procurement Work Planning And Estimation project at all?

1151. Were additional works brought about by a cause which had not previously existed?

1152. Are there regular accounting reconciliations of contract payments, transactions and inventory?

1153. When performance conditions were detailed in the tender documentation, did the contracting authority verify if the tenders received met the already stated requirements?

5.2 Contract Close-Out: Work Planning And Estimation

1154. Was the contract sufficiently clear so as not to result in numerous disputes and misunderstandings?

1155. Have all contracts been completed?

1156. How is the contracting office notified of the automatic contract close-out?

1157. Have all acceptance criteria been met prior to final payment to contractors?

1158. Parties: Authorized?

1159. Has each contract been audited to verify acceptance and delivery?

1160. Have all contracts been closed?

1161. What is capture management?

1162. What happens to the recipient of services?

1163. Have all contract records been included in the Work Planning And Estimation project archives?

1164. Was the contract complete without requiring numerous changes and revisions?

1165. Change in knowledge?

1166. Was the contract type appropriate?

1167. Are the signers the authorized officials?

1168. Change in attitude or behavior?

1169. Change in circumstances?

1170. Parties: who is involved?

1171. How does it work?

1172. How/when used ?

5.3 Project or Phase Close-Out: Work Planning And Estimation

1173. Who controlled key decisions that were made?

1174. In preparing the Lessons Learned report, should it reflect a consensus viewpoint, or should the report reflect the different individual viewpoints?

1175. Did the delivered product meet the specified requirements and goals of the Work Planning And Estimation project?

1176. What could have been improved?

1177. What information is each stakeholder group interested in?

1178. Who are the Work Planning And Estimation project stakeholders and what are roles and involvement?

1179. Planned completion date?

1180. Which changes might a stakeholder be required to make as a result of the Work Planning And Estimation project?

1181. Who is responsible for award close-out?

1182. What hierarchical authority does the stakeholder have in your organization?

1183. Were messages directly related to the release strategy or phases of the Work Planning And Estimation project?

1184. What was expected from each stakeholder?

1185. Was the user/client satisfied with the end product?

1186. What is a Risk Management Process?

1187. What information did each stakeholder need to contribute to the Work Planning And Estimation projects success?

1188. Complete yes or no?

5.4 Lessons Learned: Work Planning And Estimation

1189. How effective was Work Planning And Estimation project Team member training?

1190. What are the needs of the individuals?

1191. What were the most significant issues on this Work Planning And Estimation project?

1192. What is (are) the indicator(s) of success?

1193. How useful do individuals find communications?

1194. Where could you improve?

1195. What report generation capability is needed?

1196. Is there any way in which you think your development process hampered this Work Planning And Estimation project?

1197. Was there a Work Planning And Estimation project Definition document. Was there a Work Planning And Estimation project Plan. Were they used during the Work Planning And Estimation project?

1198. Do you conduct the engineering tests?

1199. What should have been accomplished during predeployment that was not accomplished?

1200. How effective were the communications materials in providing and orienting team members about the details of the Work Planning And Estimation project?

1201. How efficient and effective were meetings?

1202. Who needs to learn lessons?

1203. What specialization does the task require?

1204. What is the skill mix defined for the staffing?

1205. Are there any hidden conflicts of interest?

1206. For the next Work Planning And Estimation project, how could you improve on the way Work Planning And Estimation project was conducted?

1207. What is the frequency of group communications?

1208. Were any objectives unmet?

Index